UTILITY PLAYER LIFE

HOW TO PURPOSEFULLY LEVERAGE YOUR EXPERIENCE AS AN ATHLETE TO TAKE YOU WHERE YOU WANT TO GO IN LIFE.

MARTI | REED

Utility Player Life
ISBN: 978-0-578-53818-1
Copyright © 2019 by Marti Reed
www.themartireed.com

All rights reserved. No part of this book may be reproduced or transmitted in any form or by any means without written permission of the author.

Editor: Delina Pryce McPhaull

Cover Design: Justin Trawick, Justraw Creatives

Format & Layout: Chelaé Cummings, www.theblupen.com

First Edition 2019
The BluPen, LLC trade printing Manufactured and Printed in the United States of America

DEDICATION

To my parents.
Thank you for instilling a growth mindset in me, supporting me in all
I do, and setting the best example for me to follow.

To my siblings.
For always having my back and encouraging me to dream BIG.
Your love lifts me.

TABLE OF CONTENTS

INTRODUCTION..9

PART 1: THE TRANSITION
CH 1. WHY IS IT HARD FOR ATHLETES?...19
CH 2. OUR COMPETITIVE ADVANTAGE..25
CH 3. UTILITY PLAYERS THROUGHOUT HISTORY..........................29

PART 2: COMMON VALUES OF GREAT UTILITY PLAYERS
CH 4. STRENGTH OF CHARACTER..35
CH 5. FLEXIBILITY IN OPPORTUNITY..49
CH 6. STAMINA IN CREATING HABITS..59
CH 7. SPORTSMANSHIP IN LIFE...69

PART 3: UTILITY TRAINING AND POSITIONING
CH 8. BE A GOOD TEAMMATE..81
CH 9. BE A STUDENT...91
CH 10. BE AN ATHLETE..101
CH 11. BE A PROFESSIONAL...111
CH 12. BE A COMMUNITY MEMBER...129

PART 4: BUILD YOUR ROSTER
CH 13. WHY BUILD YOUR ROSTER...139
CH 14. MENTORS AND NETWORKING..145
CH 15. THE INFORMATIONAL INTERVIEW.......................................151
CH 16. MASTERMINDING...155

CLOSING..159
APPENDIX..163
ACKNOWLEDGEMENTS...169
ABOUT THE AUTHOR..173

INTRODUCTION

I grew up playing all types of sports that involved land and not water—track & field, basketball, volleyball, and softball. It was hard not to fall in love with sports having a dad that played professional baseball and being the youngest of three ultra-competitive siblings. We grew up at the park nearly every day watching my older brother play baseball, and quite naturally, I started playing softball competitively. I went on to play for my dream school, the University of California Los Angeles (UCLA) where I won a NCAA National Championship in 2010 and graduated as BruinLife's Senior of the Year in 2012. I graduated from UCLA at the top of my class and leveraged the skills I learned to land my dream job out of college — twice! I landed my first dream job as a commercial real estate broker for the largest real estate brokerage in the country, and I didn't have any real estate experience. As my dreams started to shift a few years later, I landed my next dream job as the Partnership Manager of Positive Coaching Alliance, a national non-profit devoted to teaching life lessons through sports and developing better athletes, but more importantly, better people. I started to realize that these things just didn't happen by chance. There was a systematic approach I took with what I learned through competing in sports to position myself for the success I wanted in life. I spend a lot of my time now traveling across the nation speaking to diverse audiences on how to create opportunities regardless of where you are or what life throws at you.

My formal training and involvement in sports as a player, coach and career have allowed me to see firsthand the direct power that playing sports can have on a person's life.

Sports have the power and ability to teach and build character, especially at a young age. Sports promote participation, inclusion, acceptance of rules, human values, discipline, health, tolerance, gender equality, teamwork and so many other powerful fundamentals of development.

It can teach physical character like work ethic, leadership, how to manage failure, how to deal with adversity, teamwork, sacrifice, discipline, grit, time management, responsibility, and perseverance. In sports, you learn accountability, to bounce back from mistakes, and how to win.

Beyond the physical life lessons that we learn from playing sports, we can also learn moral character — things like empathy, courage, fortitude, honesty, respect, loyalty and integrity.

All of these amazing attributes that can be gained on the playing field can be transferred over into life outside of the arena. Understanding how to make those connections and transfer the skills you learned on the playing field into your daily life will prepare you for the biggest challenges that might come your way.

A UTILITY PLAYER

Utility Player (n): A player who is capable of playing competently in any of several positions.

I grew up playing shortstop. Although I was able to play other positions as needed, I was always the shortstop on every team I played on. The shortstop was usually the position held for the most athletic person on the team. Since I had a track and basketball background, I was extremely athletic and faster than all of my softball teammates. I was the "quarterback" in the infield.

When I took my first visit to UCLA as a high school sophomore and met the current UCLA softball team for the first time and one of the players asked me, "What position do you play?" I smiled and said "shortstop." She along with a couple of the other girls on the team chuckled. With a confused look on my face I said, "What?" They all looked at me and said, "Me too." These were 3 girls on the team — one was the right fielder, one was the first baseman and one was a left fielder. None of them were the current shortstop, but they all grew up playing shortstop.

That was the first time I realized a common recruiting strategy for elite athletes. Coaches would recruit the most athletic well-rounded players, (commonly the shortstop in softball), and they would move them to whatever positions they needed them to play. The player profile on these former shortstops would list their position as "utility", meaning they played multiple positions.

Indeed, I became a utility player during my time at UCLA. I got to play the outfield and the infield — right field, second base, first base, but rarely and pretty much never, shortstop. And I was okay with it because it taught me so much more about myself and life after sports.

The most valuable people on a team are the ones that can do more than one thing well; people that excel and specialize in a few skills and expertise, but can adjust and adapt to certain situations when needed. Utility players are versatile, flexible, and are indispensable. As a utility player you have several responsibilities. As a utility player, you are always learning and growing. Although a utility player's name might not be in the headlines every day, the utility player deserves a lot of credit for a team's success.

As utility players separate themselves from the rest of the pack by developing the skills to play multiple positions, their value is immense. Just like sports call for a utility player to handle multiple responsibilities and is counted on to play any position, we all play multiple positions in life, and we must be prepared to be the utility player we're called to be.

PREPARING TO TRANSITION OUT OF SPORTS

I've heard multiple athletes say "I'd much rather take on the challenge of waking up early to run hills, lift weights, practice, study for a midterm and write a 10-page paper than have to figure out what I am supposed to do with my life after sports." It doesn't have to be this intense and scary. Utility player training can help make this transition much more exciting and liberating.

I think the worst thing athletes can do during their playing career is ignore the fact that life after sports exists. It's a real thing they need to prepare for. The transition can be made a lot smoother and easier by talking about it and planning for it ahead of time, which a lot of people don't do. Once you retire from your sport to which you dedicated your heart and passion to for the past 15 years, the sport will live on without you. You need to be prepared to take everything you learned in the sport and transition it over to your life outside of sports. This is what this book is designed to help you do.

You don't have to live in anxiety about your future and the fear of the unknown. There is a smarter game to be played. And just as you were outstanding in your sport, you can be an outstanding utility player in your life after.

MY TRANSITION

Over the summer going into my senior year at UCLA, I attended a leadership program called LEAP (Leadership Excellence Accelerating Potential). They taught us success principles that you don't normally learn in the classroom — things like networking, how to get mentors, what books to read for self-growth, how to set smart goals and achieve them, and how to manage time efficiently. During this one week program, I found the skill sets they taught me were transferable to the things I was doing my entire life through sports. I could finally see the connection clearly of how to apply these things into the real world.

I spent my senior year going to work on my personal growth (on and off of the softball field), and intentionally applying these skills and advantages I had as an athlete into my career and development search.

I woke up an hour earlier and read books about business and growth. I planned my day in the mornings and was on top of all of my assignments. I wrote down daily, weekly and monthly goals and I would read them out loud. I had a clear vision of where I was going and how to get there. I was a completely different person — a better person.

We had Mondays off for practice, and every Monday I would sit down for coffee, breakfast or lunch with a new mentor — someone that did something or was doing something in their life that I was even remotely interested in, and was willing to teach me how they did it. I asked them questions. At LEAP they call this the "informational interview." I went around every week interviewing people — professors, my parent's friends, my teammates' parents, anyone I could find, and they were so willing to help me by just lending me 30 minutes to an hour of their time to answer questions about what they did for a living, how they got there, and any advice they would give to a college student looking to get started in their career path.

I also asked them what books they read, courses they took, and who they looked up to and learned from. I would take their advice and put it into action in my life. I remember being on the bus traveling to away tournaments and games with my team, and during the ride I would be reading books like *Think and Grow Rich* by Napoleon Hill, or *How to Win Friends and Influence People* by Dale Carnegie. My teammates would make fun of me (out of love). They'd laugh and say things like, "Really, Marti? Are you going to teach us how to win friends and influence people?"

I was one of the most outgoing people on the team and wasn't struggling at all to make friends. If you really know me, you would think I should be the last one reading a book about how to build relationships. I found that the book wasn't just about how to win friends. It was a book that challenged my thinking and helped me grow and get better at the things I was pretty good at already. I always say, "You don't have to be sick to get better." I was learning that I always had something new to learn.

I went through that year as a master in learning, not just from myself, but from others. This gained me a world of knowledge, insights and wisdom. By the time I graduated, I had interviewed nearly 50 people. By graduation, I had people calling me offering me jobs and internships. I graduated from UCLA and immediately went on a carefree cruise to

Mexico, knowing I had the luxury and freedom to choose from a list of options and offers for where I wanted to work next waiting for me when I returned.

Meanwhile, all of my friends and teammates were freaking out about what they were going to do after graduation and how to start their life after sports. I started receiving Facebook messages from other former athletes asking me questions.

"How did you find a job?"

"How did you know what you wanted to do after sports? I am so scared; can you help me?"

"What did you do to get where you are so quickly?"

Message after message kept pouring in and at that point, I knew my athlete community needed help. I knew that this was something that needed to be taught and shared with others.

I once heard a speaker say something that has stuck with me until this day. He said that being aware is a gift. Once you've been given the gift of awareness, it lacks integrity to not share the gift of awareness with others. So, as I am now aware of how to leverage the skills I've learned on the playing field to take me where I want to go in life after sports, it is my duty to share this awareness with the rest of you. We can all be utility players in life.

On a tangible level, I wrote this book to show athletes how to become a utility player in their life and leverage their experience as an athlete to help them grow in their career. As an athlete, we work on our strength, flexibility, stamina and sportsmanship. This book is similar, but the approach focuses on the training we do off the playing field and the transferable skills we can use in life. With an athletic foundation, this book surpasses the athletic arena and will reach audiences of all types. The purpose of this book is to help people reach their full potential. This book will help you identify and create opportunities regardless of where you are or what life throws at you. Anyone who is passionate, competitive, and looking to reach another level in their life while maintaining a balance in all the positions they play, this book will help them do so. To be at the top of your game in life, you must dedicate yourself to daily exercises that will build a positive mindset, develop your network, and give back to your community. I will include "Utility Workouts" at the end of most chapters, or actionable and tangible items you can do and implement in your life right away. These activities can be done individually or in group settings with a team. There's a saying that knowledge is power, but the truth is, knowledge is potential power. We must turn knowledge into action and do something with it! The point of the Utility Workouts is to turn your knowledge into action. You will play multiple positions in life. When you are prepared for all of them, you are ready for bigger, better successes than you can even imagine. Not only will this book motivate and encourage you, this book will help you grow in your life immensely. Thanks for taking this journey with me!

PART 1

THE TRANSITION

CHAPTER 1

Why Is It Hard for Athletes?

Athletes are trained to push through pain, outlast hardships and endure sacrifices as the price they must pay for victory and achievement. Athletes are accustomed to going through tough times, putting in hard work, doing whatever it takes (even if that means temporary suffering) to reach an end goal. The trade-off along the way are things you can't even quantify — like the shared experience with other athletes, teammates, coaches and supporters.

In sports we learn that when we put in "X" we'll get "Y" in return. For athletes, the playing field is a comfortable and familiar place to be because we're prepared, acclimated to the pressure, and passionate about our sport.

But what happens when the stadium lights are turned off on our playing careers and when the fans find someone new to cheer for?

What happens when our playing time is up and we are no longer in our comfort zones, and now have to tackle life after sports?

What happens when the time comes for us to hang up our cleats, the cheering stops, and kids are no longer asking for our autograph?

What happens when everything you've known and what's become your identity is suddenly stripped away and you have to build and recreate a new identity?

This is what athletes face when it's time to retire. This is why most athletes face an identity crisis when they no longer play their sport. All college students have to go into that transition from college to the real world, but collegiate athletes feel this transition the hardest.

When I played sports in college, it was my "job." Students that weren't athletes had time to work traditional jobs and internships, and gain work experience while they studied in school. It was intimidating, having been a full-time athlete for the majority of my life, realizing that I would have to find a way to be a "normal person" and navigate life after sports.

For many athletes, especially those who were among the best in their sport, it is hard to admit that you're afraid and that you struggle in the transition from sports to the real world. Being an elite athlete and then having to transition to a beginner in another area, is a truly humbling experience. Most of us are not ready for that transition.

Who wants to go from being an expert (elite athlete) to a beginner sales rep for a large company? There will be a learning curve. Many times, it will be a steep learning curve. Your ego will want to protect itself from the frightening reality that things have changed. It will take time for your mind and heart to adjust to the fact that you might have a while to go to get back at the

YOU MUST LEARN TO ADJUST AND ADAPT TO CHANGE.

top in this new arena. You will no longer be the shining star. And although you won't necessarily doubt that you will make it, you will just have less control over when you'll be back at the top again. And as a former athlete, I know that control is something you are used to. Like I mentioned before, we are used to when we put in "X", we'll get "Y" in return. Athletes are used to seeing the end goal clearly and it makes sense.

In the real world, one might put in "X" and not get "Y" in return (at least not right when you expect it). The outcome is less inside of your control and that can be scary. But if making it to the top of your sport is tough, why shouldn't transcending into a successful life after sports be any different? It's immature to think that your new circumstances will just adapt to you. Immature people think, "If things go my way, then I'm feeling great and I'm really happy. But if circumstances don't go my way, then I'm miserable and I will let everyone know it."

During this transition, we must learn to adjust and adapt, rather than sit around waiting for something to change and adapt to us. Just like in sports where we were in control of our next move, we have to realize that in life, our efforts will also make a difference.

As athletes growing up playing a sport, we developed the passion and confidence naturally — our skills improved and we experienced wins and victories along the way. As we developed the abilities, we weren't constantly questioning the process. We knew exactly what to expect. In life after sports, it can be the opposite. This can be extremely tough for athletes.

In life after sports, athletes are constantly questioning what they're interested in, where their strengths lie and attempting to create new confidence in a hostile environment where they are often working their way up from the bottom.

In the summer of 2016, one of my teammates from college took a group of us to Lake Arrowhead for some fun water activities. The group was made up of former athletes—former softball and football players. We had never wake-boarded before.

I tried so many times to get up from the water, but I kept falling down into the water. The boat would go, and I would try to stand and I would get yanked over and face plant, or I would let go of the line, or fall to the side. I was trying my hardest to just stand and ride the wave but I had no idea what I was doing, and I just kept getting more and more frustrated and exhausted after every failed attempt. You should have seen me in that water, punching it (as if I could hurt it) with frustration! My football friends tried too and they also couldn't get up on the water. They were getting just as mad. After hours of failed attempts, we all got back in the boat, defeated by this new sport. All we could do was laugh at each other! I was the first to admit, "I'm not used to being that bad at something, and it sucks!" All of my friends agreed.

The transition from sports to the real world can make feelings of inadequacy surface. For an athlete, we often feel it on a deeper level. We are having to rebuild our identity and self-worth to adapt to new challenges and environments that we've never encountered before. That's tough!

I've found that a successful transition for athletes to the real world takes about two years on average, while an unsuccessful one can take a lifetime. Two years might seem like a long time, but think about how long it takes for a young aspiring athlete to transition into an elite level player — probably 5 to 10 years. In comparison, it's really not that long. In those two years, you will be navigating and adapting to multiple changes in your life — career, financial, interpersonal, physical, and mental. Just one massive change in one of these areas would take a good amount of adjustment time, let alone facing these changes all at once. It can be very overwhelming, which is why it can often lead to depression or at the very least, wishing you could turn back time to be a student-athlete all over again.

Keeping the challenges of transition to ourselves and refusing to admit they are real can imprison us in our own thoughts and make things much harder in the long run. We are trained in the world of athletics to believe things like injury are a form of weakness. Those beliefs can screw us up mentally — making it hard to ask for help in life after sports.

It's okay to feel lost or not know what you are going to do next. It's okay to feel the uncertainty of what the future holds. You are not alone. In this time of vulnerability, understand that you don't have to go about it on your own. You can ask for help and take time to discover your purpose beyond the playing field.

Have you ever come back from behind in a tough game? This is the time to remember comeback moments. Remember the times when there was doubt and uncertainty and you never gave up. You stuck to the plan and made it out on top. Just like competing in sports and overcoming challenges that you didn't think you could, you are made for the challenge of conquering life after sports. You have a competitive advantage.

CHAPTER 2

Our Competitive Advantage

I have always believed that playing sports for most of my life gave me an advantage for when I walk into any room. My background in sports gives me the confidence I need to approach others, to step out of my comfort zone, to try something new.

I have always known how much athletics boosts my self-esteem and confidence. As a little girl, I was a huge introvert and often was picked on and bullied for being a tomboy or wearing glasses at the age of four. I struggled with finding the courage to open my mouth and speak to people. Even a simple "hello!" was hard for me to get out. As a result, I didn't have many friends before I started playing organized sports. Playing sports helped break me out of my shell and allowed me to be comfortable in my own skin and communicate with others. Today I am an outgoing, talkative, public speaker. It's clear that playing sports has completely helped shape me into the person I am.

What do many CEO's have in common? They played sports when they were younger. Let's take an inside look at some former athletes who used their competitive edge to transition into executive positions.

Walter Robb, former CEO of the renowned supermarket chain Whole Foods was the captain of the Stanford Soccer Team.

Jeffrey Immelt, who retired CEO of General Electric, played football at Dartmouth. He attributes his success in business to what he learned in sports. "Not every play works…but you've got to figure it out, and there's always a next play. And I think all of those things just happen to stick with you…in my case for my whole life. This essence of trying to build a culture of excellence that I learned in sports I very much brought to the business world."

Brian Moynihan, the chairman and CEO of Bank of America was a rugby player at Brown University.

Former chairman and CEO of IBM, Samuel Palmisano, played football for Johns Hopkins and walked away from an NFL tryout with the Raiders to pursue a sales job.

Brian Roberts, chairman and CEO of Comcast Corporation competed in squash at the University of Pennsylvania, and won a gold medal for the US Squash team.

Before becoming General Motors CEO from 2010 to 2014, Daniel Akerson boxed at the Naval Academy.

Even Mark Zuckerberg, co-founder and CEO of Facebook was a high school fencing star.

It's even more common for female executives to have played a sport at some point in their lives. According to the 2013 Ernst & Young study after surveying 821 high-level executives, they found that 90 percent of the women sampled played sport. This amount rose to 96 percent among women currently in a C-suite position.

Meg Whitman, CEO of Hewlett-Packard (commonly referred to as HP and probably what you use for printing) was the captain of the swim team and also played varsity lacrosse, tennis and basketball in high school. She was also on both the squash and lacrosse teams at Princeton University.

Lynn Elsenhans, the chairman and CEO of Sunoco until 2012, was a member of Rice University's first ever women's intercollegiate basketball team before she became the first woman to run a major oil company.

PepsiCo CEO Indra Nooyi played cricket in college.

Irene Rosenfeld played basketball at Cornell University and is now the CEO and chairwoman of Mondelēz International, the multinational candy, food and beverage company.

As you can see, there is a common trend here. Does playing sports guarantee you success in life? No. Playing sports and life success are not causation, but correlation. And once you understand the correlation, it will lead you to bigger and better things that you've ever imagined.

CHAPTER 3

Utility Players Throughout History

Throughout history there have been multiple examples of utility players who have paved the way and made a mark for others to do the same.

One of my favorite athletes and heroes, Jackie Robinson is the perfect example of a utility player. Jackie Robinson's legacy goes way beyond his epic contributions to the sport of baseball. This legend was showing up in his community long before he integrated the sport in 1947. Eleven years before Rosa Parks declined to give up her seat aboard a Montgomery bus, Jackie Robinson refused to give up his seat aboard a Camp Hood bus when he was in the military. The incident led to a court martial in which Robinson was acquitted. One year after Robinson broke the color barrier in baseball, President Harry S. Truman ordered the desegregation of the military. Jackie Robinson is not only one of the greatest athletes of all time, he was the first athlete to letter in four varsity sports at UCLA: track & field, football, basketball, and baseball. He was also recognized as a major influence to the non-violent U.S. Civil Rights movement.

UTILITY PLAYERS SHOW UP BEYOND SPORTS

Abraham Lincoln, one of the most influential men of our country is another example of a utility player. Although he was exceptional with an axe, and competed in wrestling matches with his tall, strong athletic figure, his impact was beyond any athletic arena. The ultimate utility player is able to create opportunities regardless of where they are and what life throws at them. Lincoln did just that.

Born into poverty and humble beginnings, Lincoln's work ethic, self-discipline and optimism allowed him to pave his own way. Lincoln was one of the best problem-solvers this nation has ever seen. Before he was named the 16th President of the United States, he invented a system (in which he holds a patent) that helps a stuck ship over obstacles. Lincoln established the U.S. Department of Agriculture, signed the first of the Homestead Acts allowing poor people to obtain land, the Morril Land-Grant Act which led to the creation of numerous universities, established the progressive nature of income tax and the U.S. National Banking System, and he issued the Emancipation Proclamation which led to the abolishing of slavery in the U.S. Oh yeah, and let's not forget him leading the Union to victory in the American Civil War. Beyond these accomplishments, he is known as "Honest Abe" for his impeccable character and integrity. Talk about playing multiple positions and having an impact; the life Lincoln lived is one to never forget.

Earvin (Magic) Johnson is another utility player in life who has set the bar for what life can be after sports. This Hall of Fame basketball player did not let the sport of basketball define him. He used his influential platform to recreate his brand from basketball star to business investor and entrepreneurial star. After courageously announcing he had HIV and retiring from the game, going back to the game and playing some more, then retiring again, he built a business empire that includes real estate, restaurants, sports teams, poultry, and more!

I had the pleasure of getting to know Magic personally when I was in college after I was selected (four times) as a Taylor Michael Scholar through his Magic Johnson Foundation. He taught me some of the greatest life lessons of a utility player. He attributes his success to building his roster, finding the right mentors, and always approaching life as a student willing to learn from others.

In 1990, Magic purchased the Pepsi-Cola distribution plant in Forestville, Maryland with the help and mentorship of Black Enterprise publisher, Earl G. Graves. He found the right mentor who believed in him and was willing to teach him the ropes, which eventually led to the start of Johnson Development Corporation in 1992 which brought movie theaters into minority communities. The rest is history! The coolest part about Magic's business and life success is he plays the position of community member very well, always finding ways to improve and build in the communities where there is a lack of resources, funds and opportunity.

Ronda Rousey is also living the utility player life. She understands that competing as a top UFC martial arts athlete is only one part of her impact, and as a utility player, she serves other positions in her life. "It's not your purpose in life to be happy; it's your purpose in life to leave this world better than how you found it," she said. She is one of the most charitable athletes, most actively involved in the Didi Hirsch campaign to provide mental health services in communities where stigma and poverty limit access. Ronda has also worked with the UN's Free Rice Campaign and founded Gomper's Middle School Judo Program.

There are tons more examples and I can go on and on about the utility players throughout history and today, but I think you get the picture. Utility players in life are able to leverage the skills they learn out on the playing field to take them where they want to go beyond their athletic abilities. Utility players show up in so many areas of life with the same competitive drive they learned from sports. In order to be a utility player in life, you have to have a strong foundation to build upon. Next we'll explore what are the common values of utility players and how you can build those core values in your life as well.

PART 2

COMMON VALUES OF GREAT UTILITY PLAYERS

CHAPTER 4

Strength of Character

The character of an individual is much more than their reputation or what meets the eye. The character of an individual is made up of the moral distinct qualities, which can be determined by the way they act and respond regardless of the circumstance or who is watching.

UTILITY PLAYERS FOCUS ON BUILDING STRENGTH OF CHARACTER!

Simply put, your character is your inner-most self; the things that are at your core. Our core values are our sacred truths; the things that define us. Core values are principles that shape the fundamental beliefs of how we behave towards others, as well as ourselves, in pursuit of our purpose. Who are you when no one is watching? What are the things, beliefs, and attitudes that you value?

I am guided by my faith, family, opportunities to grow and service to others. Those four principles are the foundation that helps guide my decision-making process as I pursue my purpose. The things I value at my core are integrity, loyalty, courage, positive attitude, health, respect, hard work, gratitude and servant leadership. I try to surround myself with those that have similar values and guiding principles.

In life after sports, the character of an individual is one of the most important transferable qualities. Character is the foundation of your life that you build upon. It is the solid ground that you will be able to stand on when things get tough or when life's challenging moments are putting you to the test. Sports are a beautiful opportunity to build character.

John Wooden, who's considered to be one of the greatest coaches of all time, said, "The true test of a man's character is what he does when nobody's watching." Under conditions of encouragement, challenge, and support, sports provide opportunities to pursue excellence of character. Athletic excellence takes courage, immaculate dedication, honesty, leadership, respect, hard work and perseverance. These things are not only built on game day, but often in times when no one is watching, there's no immediate reward, or when you don't feel like doing it. Some of the best advice I received as an athlete was from Carol Dweck's book, *Mindset*. She describes two types of mindsets that we develop; a growth mindset and a fixed mindset. A fixed mindset assumes that things like our talent, abilities and our character is static, set and can't be changed. On the other hand, a growth mindset believes that ability is learned, developed and changeable, not fixed or set in stone. A growth mindset thrives on challenge and sees failure as a boost to growth. It's not about your circumstance, it's not even about your talent, it's about your grit.

Anything life-long utility players wish to do, they can do it if they work hard and learn to bounce back from failure. Nothing is fixed or set in stone. Failure isn't fixed. Ability isn't fixed. Everything is learned and earned. It's developed by growth.

As utility players, it is extremely fruitful to approach life as a learner. The more you learn, the more you grow and the better equipped you will be to make decisions. Having a solid personal philosophy will help you see (and minimize) the dangers, as well as see (and maximize) the opportunities. In Hal Elrod's book, *The Miracle Morning* (a must read), he talks about how our personal philosophy and development are so important because our lives are not our circumstances. Our lives are much more than our current "life situation." I truly believe our internal structures, attitudes, and beliefs can give us the power to adjust, enhance, or change our life situation at any given moment. Simply put, our outer world is a reflection of our inner world. In the words of the great rhymester and lyricist Lauryn Hill, "How you gon' win when you ain't right within?...nuh uh. Come again." Bottom line—it all boils down to character.

Your character may have been tested in sports, but even more so, it will be tested when you're off the playing field.

Character is often tested when you are outside of your comfort zone. Having true solid character will help you stay the course when things get hard. Having solid character will give you the strength you need when circumstances make you weak. Having a bulletproof character will not only help you grow and thrive to where you want to go, but help you stay at the top once you make it there.

One of my favorite quotes is by the great coach John Wooden, "Be more concerned with your character than your reputation, because your character is what you really are, while your reputation is merely what others think you are." I think that it would be very naïve for me to say "who cares what other people think of you" because most of us do care what others think, even when we say we don't. I'm speaking authentically as a true learner in life, and someone who often has to remind herself not to worry about what others will think and say of me if I am being true to myself.

The truth is, it's not easy to not worry or feel anything about how others think of us. We can receive validation, praise, accountability and guidance from others, and often look to others for that stability in our lives. And it doesn't feel good not to be loved by others, so I think it is human nature to want to feel accepted. People don't judge who we actually are, they judge who they think we are or who we've led them to believe we are. And the more time and effort that we put into letting others believe we're something other than our authentic selves, the longer and harder the fall when the truth comes out. And trust me, the truth will eventually come out.

The true issue behind worrying about what others think of us is we seek validation and love and support from the wrong people; people that we don't know well and vice versa; people that don't even belong on our roster (I will dedicate an entire section in this book on what it means to build your "roster," but for now, think of it as your personal "team"). It's okay to want others to respect you and think well of you, but you have to desire this validation from the right people —those you respect. The people who belong on your roster are the people that you love—those who help shape you into the person you are and the person you're becoming. Focus on the reputation you're building with those on your roster. Don't let the opinion of others beyond that core group, carry a lot of weight. It's your character that counts. When the time comes to transfer from the athletic arena to the real world, it's your character that's going to give you the strength you need to make this transition with integrity.

CHARACTER SHAPES IDENTITY

I remember hearing a story in Sunday school at church when I was a young girl, which has stuck with me throughout the years. I remember it like this:

One day a king came out to his garden and saw withering and dying trees, bushes and flowers. An oak tree said, "I am dying because I can't be as high as a pine." As he walked closer to the pine tree, it said, "I'm falling down because I can't give grapes like a grapevine." The grapevine said it was dying because it couldn't blossom like a rose. Soon the king found a single plant with beautiful flowers — pleasing the heart, bloomy and fresh. The king asked, "All the trees and flowers here are withering, and you are flourishing. Why?" The plant replied, "I think it comes naturally. I believe that when you planted me, you wanted to get a joy plant. If you had wanted to grow an oak, grapes or a rose, you would have planted them. So, I think that I can't be anything else than what I am, and I stick to developing my best qualities.

The joy plant taught me to focus on developing and using my best qualities, and not to worry about the qualities that others had.

The most beautiful thing about you is the fact that you are YOU. There are so many people, things and concepts in society that will try to shape you into something that you are not. It is so easy to get distracted by outside sources. As soon as you start focusing on what others have and who others are, you'll start to lose sight of who you are. I'm guilty of it too. But I am here to remind you to be true to yourself and be true to who you are because you are enough.

Who you are is where your gift lies, and when you're being your unique authentic self, people can relate to you. When you accept who you are, you can allow yourself to grow and blossom, or you can go with who society tells you to be and wither.

We must realize that when we're sharing that unique gift of our true selves, there will be some people that don't like it or don't agree with it. When you put yourself out there, you will be judged regardless of how good or bad you are. Every time I hit post on a blog or story, I'm opening myself up to be judged by the world. But I am constantly reminding myself, "You can't please everyone, and the first step to being unhappy is trying to please the world."

Take a look at where you are right now in your life. Are you being true to yourself? In that career? In that relationship? In the major that you chose in school? Are you doing it because it's who you are and it's what you want? Or are you listening to what outside sources are telling you to do in order to please others? Don't stay in it for others. Don't stay in it to please society. Public perception isn't worth losing yourself. Your future is in good hands. Yes, there will be doubters and naysayers, but when you are true to yourself, the right people will love and support you, and everybody else will just have to deal with your greatness. What would your life look like if you focused more on your character and less on your reputation?

When I was a real estate broker, working 60-hour weeks and aggressively climbing the corporate ladder, I told myself a story. And in my story, I could not separate my identity from my corporate dream.

I believed: "I am my job, I am my career, I am my company. I am supposed to go down this path. I am not meant to go down the path of uncertainty." I told myself that it was okay to be miserable now so I could maybe be happy one day in the future —and I married that story in a match made in hell. The day I decided to stop resisting and to start being truly honest with myself, was the day my life changed for the better. I asked myself a tough, but reviving question that we all need to ask ourselves more often when faced with decisions, opportunities, and detours:

Why am I doing this, really? What's the real reason why I am doing this?

We don't ask ourselves this question enough because it can be a very convicting, uncomfortable question to answer. And to be honest, a lot of times we don't even want to know the answer. If you want to make the right decision and look back to a defining moment in your life and say "wow, I am so happy I did that," you have to start by asking yourself "why am I doing the things that I am doing?"

In every transition in your life, in every decision-making environment, you are writing the story of your life that you want to tell. We all have a story up to this point of where we are in life, but when we're faced with new defining decisions and moments, we have to consider which of these decisions, which of these choices is most consistent with the story we've been telling so far, and the story we want to tell in the future?

A very wise man once told me that the next season of your life is nothing more (no matter how big or scary or uncertain it is) than a story that one day you're going to tell.

You want to be able to tell your whole story. You're going to want to be able to look the person you fall in love with in the eye and tell them your whole story without having to lie about who you are. You're going to want to be able to look your future kid in the eye and be proud of the story you tell. Whenever you are faced with a new decision, a choice, an opportunity, ask yourself, "What is the story I want to someday tell?" and use that to help guide you in the right direction.

> **PERSONAL DEVELOPMENT COMES BEFORE THE FORTUNE!**

Every one of us has a story to tell. The question now becomes, is your story empowering you to maximize what God has given to you, or is your story causing you to fall short?

Personal development or the development of your character is so important because your life is a result of not only the value you bring, but the value you become, and what you become matters much more than what you bring. Renowned speaker and author Jim Rohn said, "personal development comes before the fortune." And "fortune" doesn't necessarily mean money and wealth. It can also mean relationships, health, profession, education, family, marriage—whatever it is that you are building or growing towards in your life.

"Our level of success will rarely exceed our level of personal development, because success is something we attract by who we become." - Jim Rohn

Jim Rohn taught me to go to work on myself harder than I work on my job (and I work very hard on my job). He said if you work hard on your job, you can make a living (which is fine), but if you work hard on yourself, you can make a fortune (which is super-fine). You don't have to work on the economy. Become an attractive person to the marketplace and the economy will adjust to you. Your income is determined by your philosophy. Go to work on yourself to make yourself more valuable and more ready for money making opportunities that come your way.

Let me put this in another context for those that may not understand. Do you know anyone that's so desperate to be in a happy relationship? You know, that one friend that's always talking about marriage or pursuing a mate? Well guess what, the best time to prepare for that relationship is before you're in one. So instead of focusing on pursuing a mate, tell your friend to focus on becoming the right mate for the right person. Then they will attract the right person in their lives.

Here are some ways to develop yourself and your character:

LEARN FROM PERSONAL EXPERIENCE—THE TRIAL AND ERROR METHOD

All the things you've done wrong in your life can contribute to the person you become. They can make you better if you learn from them, or they can make you worse if you continue doing them over and over while expecting different results (definition of insanity).

PAY ATTENTION—SUCCESS LEAVES CLUES

Be a better observer of the people doing well and the people falling behind and take mental notes and adjust to what you're doing based on what you see. Whether negative or positive, the experiences of others can help you get to where you want to be. You can avoid mistakes by watching what other people do wrong and not making the same mistakes they did, and you can create opportunities by watching what other people do right and asking them to teach you how they did it. This is the strategy I lean on the most. Who are you learning from?

READ, READ, AND READ SOME MORE

There are so many books (audio and hard copies) that can change the course of your life. Most people don't read because they "don't have time." No one has time. You make time. Wake up an hour earlier. Listen to audio books while driving. I read every day for about 20 - 30 minutes and I get through 2 books a month (and my mentors tell me that's still not enough). Trust me, you've got to make this a priority, or you won't do it. When you read, sort through, gather information and decide what is valuable to try, then go apply the things you learn. I'll mention my favorite books throughout this book, but my go to, life changing, must reads are *Think & Grow Rich* by Napoleon Hill, *How to Win Friends & Influence People* by Dale Carnegie, *The 5 Love Languages* by Gary Chapman, *Who Moved My Cheese* by Spencer Johnson, and *The 7 Habits of Highly Effective People* by Stephen Covey.

In order for us to reach our potential and to create the levels of personal, professional, and financial success that we desire, we must first commit to dedicating time each and every day to becoming the person we need to be; one who is qualified and capable of consistently attracting, creating and sustaining the life we want. Who you're becoming is far more important than what you're doing, and yet it's what you're doing that is determining who you're becoming. Work to improve yourself every day.

PRESSURE AND CHALLENGE

As athletes, we understand how to deal with pressure. We are faced with high-pressure moments in game-time situations often. Have you ever missed the game-winning shot? Or dropped the ball when everyone was counting on you? Being able to perform when the stakes are high and the challenge is vast only makes us better competitors. Without challenge, without pressure, without obstacles, what is there to overcome? Learning to work through high pressure moments as athletes prepares us for high-pressure moments in life outside of sports.

Our character is built in moments of pressure. When we are deeply challenged in life, it is an opportunity to grow and strengthen our character. Challenges and disappointments are going to happen; it's inevitable. No matter how rich, wealthy, talented or gifted you are, no one is exempt from heartache, pain, disappointment, and hurt. We are all subject to pressure and challenges in life, but it's the way we respond and learn from those challenges that makes us strong. The problems of life, as difficult as they can be, always have a purpose behind them. There's always a lesson to be learned. I believe we were all created in the image of Jesus Christ, who is perfect. Building character is a constant effort of chipping away the things within us that don't look like Jesus. Sometimes God allows distractions in our lives or little irritations to help rub off the rough edges of our character. Other times, we might face a huge jackhammer of a challenge that has the ability to chip away huge chunks of our character that don't look like Jesus. If we embrace the problems we face as opportunities to grow in Christ's image, and strengthen our character, then we will have less room for worry, doubt, feeling sorry for ourselves, or getting angry.

UTILITY WORKOUTS

At the end of each chapter moving forward, I will include "Utility Workouts" or actionable items you can implement in your life right away. These activities can be done individually or in group settings with a team. There's a saying that knowledge is power, but the truth is, knowledge is potential power. We must turn knowledge into action and do something with it! The point of the utility workouts is to turn your knowledge into action.

LIVE A LIFE OF PURPOSE
If you were receiving the lifetime achievement award, what would your award say?

DEFINE YOUR CORE VALUES
Use the Core Values chart on the next page and choose your top 3 in each category. Then narrow those 3 down to one in each category. Turn your core value into an actionable statement. How will you practice this value? How can you measure your progress with this value? (This list is just to get you started. Feel free to add your own words that aren't on the list)

SPIRITUAL	SOCIAL RELATIONSHIPS	EDUCATION CAREER	PHYSICAL HEALTH
Honest	Family	Motivated	Healthy
Humble	Friendly	Wealthy	Physically Fit
Giving	Cheerful	Ambitious	Attractive
Unselfish	Popular	Hard Worker	Clean
Trustworthy	Enthusiastic	Educated	Eat Right
Grateful	Cooperative	Dependable	Good Athlete
Forgiving	Patient	Positive Attitude	Active
Brave	Pleasing	Extra Mile	Strong
Faithful	Likable	Reliable	
Trusting	Kind	Consistent	
Peaceful	Thoughtful	Respected	
	Good Listener	Results Oriented	
	Outgoing	Accurate	
	Energetic	Team Player	
	Loving		
	Acceptance		
	Humor		

SPIRITUAL: (i.e. I will remain grateful for the opportunities, people and things I have in my life.) _____
_____
_____

SOCIAL/RELATIONSHIPS: (i.e. I am enthusiastic, and I lift up others with my positive energy.) _____
_____
_____

EDUCATION/CAREER: (i.e. I am a hard worker giving consistent effort in school and work.) _____

_____

_____

PHYSICAL/HEALTH: (i.e. I am physically active and committed to living a healthy life.) _____

_____

_____

FIND CHARACTER ROLE MODELS

Make a list from one to five. Name the character traits for which you would like to be remembered. Next to each character trait, write the name of someone in your life who you believe possesses this character trait. Reach out to that person and ask them how they've been able to build that trait in their life.

PRESSURE BUILDS CHARACTER

In what area of your life are you currently experiencing the most pressure? How have you responded to this so far, and how might this be an opportunity to build your character?

CHAPTER 5

Flexibility in Opportunity

During a panel discussion, a student asked me, "Marti, how do you find the time to prepare yourself for all of the things you end up doing, and the opportunities you've had in your life?" That's a great question.

Can I be transparent with you? Good, because here's my answer: I've become comfortable with being uncomfortable. I know it sounds a little contradictory, but it's the truth. My coach used to always tell us, "You have to get comfortable with being uncomfortable." Playing softball and coming off of the bench in the middle of a close game to pinch hit, which means subbing into a game that you haven't played in yet, but being expected to perform with consistency is an uncomfortable situation. I would face those challenges head-on and never back down. And the more comfortable I got in those uncomfortable situations, the stronger I was in the long run.

In my life after sports, I haven't always felt comfortable and fully prepared for each of the opportunities that have come my way. I'm a bit of a perfectionist, so even though others may have thought I was ready, I didn't feel I was on the level of preparation I liked to be on before doing something. In other words, I am not always comfortable with my ability to do something before I do it, but I do it anyway. And that, my friends, is one of the main reasons I've been able to accomplish a number of things in my life.

UTILITY PLAYERS HAVE GREAT FLEXIBILITY IN OPPORTUNITY

During the summer of 2013 I received an email from the Magic Johnson Foundation asking me if I would speak with Mr. Earvin Magic Johnson himself at their TMSP Program (which is the scholarship program for his foundation) on the topic of Networking Strategies. I was a recent grad of his program and only one year out of college. They were known to bring in guest speakers like the CEO of FedEx, or the president of IBM, in other words, seasoned executives. So you can understand why my initial reaction was, "this must be a mistake." I even called the Magic Johnson Foundation and asked them if they accidentally sent me an email about speaking at the conference. They assured me that it was no mistake and they needed to know as soon as possible if I was available because the conference was coming up in a few days.

Immediately my heart dropped and my mind started racing with terrible thoughts. I'm not prepared. I don't have enough time. There's no way I can do this. Why should these students even listen to me? Who am I? OMG, if I mess up, I'm going to look so stupid! Oh snap! And not only will I look stupid, even worse, I'm going to make Magic look stupid! Oh no, this ain't good. They better call somebody else.

I was uncomfortable and felt unprepared and under-qualified. I was not being a flexible utility player. I was in my head, ready to hold myself back from one of the greatest opportunities that would come to change my life.

We all have insecurities. Mine was the notion that I was too young, and under-qualified to speak in front of my peers with my mentor and business idol. But thank the Lord I didn't let these doubts get in the way of saying "yes" to this opportunity. I accepted and ended up doing a great job.

Utility players understand that opportunities often come when we least expect them. Don't miss your destiny or your breakthrough opportunities because of your own insecurities. We can spend more time thinking of the reasons why it won't work instead of how it can. In my moment of weakness, instead of finding solutions, I made excuses. How many times have you backed out of an opportunity because of something inside telling you that you weren't good enough, or you couldn't do it? Or maybe there's a past failure or mishap in your life that's haunting you and making you feel inadequate for the things that are happening now? Everyone has that special "it" they're chasing after, whether "it" is health, wealth, relationships, friendships, or school, if you want "it" bad enough, it is possible. But it's extremely hard to accomplish things if you don't get out of your own way first.

The self-limiting thoughts and beliefs in your head are what's holding you back from reaching your success. Your gifts will only be used to the extent of your willingness. No more excuses. Whatever your circumstance may be, it is not the reason for why you are not where you want to be in life, because people with far less have achieved much more. Often times we are called to opportunities before we're ready. The possibility for embarrassment and greatness coexist in the same space. True growth and great accomplishment happen when you push yourself out of your comfort zone, become flexible and get comfortable with being uncomfortable.

Back in 2012 I was working for a large commercial real estate company and building my own real estate business by leveraging their platform, working over 60 hours a week, hustling the phones with cold calls, and putting myself through distress for the sake of the dolla, dolla, dolla bills y'all! I had built my 10-year-plan to be financially free through brokerage, but didn't realize that I wasn't living to my potential or listening to the vision that God placed in my heart. I figured if I could just grind it out (even if towards something I wasn't passionate about), I'd be able to make money fast, and live my passionate dream later. PAUSE!

LIFE IS TOO SHORT TO WAIT TO USE YOUR GIFTS, AND NOT FOLLOW YOUR DREAMS

So finally, I realized that the brokerage business was not for me, which was only half of the battle in the process of living my purpose. I then had to make a decision to act and commit to living my dream by making a change.

In order to step out of my comfort zone and change my life, I followed these simple steps:

1. PRAY

I am a devout Christian, so I always look to God for the answers first before making any big decisions in my life. I gave my undivided attention to my Creator and asked for the answers and spiritual guidance through my journey, making sure my decision to change my career path was one rooted in Christ and would ultimately glorify Him over anything else. Once you hear from God, you must step out on faith and trust that He will see you through.

2. RESEARCH

I did my homework. I read books on motivation, business, self-growth, finances, you name it! I am constantly reading and learning from books daily. I also learn from other people's experiences. I spoke to mentors, or people who had been there, done that, and are STILL doing it, that could help me make better decisions on the direction in my career and my life.

3. TRUST YOUR GUT

In the end I knew that no one but me had the power to change the situation I was in. It was ultimately my decision to move forward. I knew that if I didn't see it in my heart or mind first, then I would never see it manifest in my reality. So I had to trust in what I was feeling inside and fully commit to going for it.

4. ACT

Like I mentioned earlier, everyone always says, "Knowledge is power" and that saying is wrong! Knowledge is only potential power. I can read all the books in the world, and talk to all the people in the world, but if I don't put what I learn into action, then it is a waste of knowledge. I jumped out of my comfort zone and resigned from the commercial real estate company where I was working in order to devote my life to the dreams that God placed in my heart.

I challenge you to step out of your comfort zone and have the courage and strength to walk away from people and opportunities that no longer serve your purpose.

Another way to remain flexible with the opportunities in your life is to focus on the things you can control. Have you ever been driving on the freeway on a mission to get somewhere and then BAM! Traffic hits? You're instantly in a foul mood. *"NOOO! Seriously?! Why today?!"*

Well let's think for a second here. The traffic is out of your control. You can't do anything about it, right? You can't sprinkle fairy dust and make the traffic disappear. Instead of sitting there upset and hurt about it, why not say "it is what it is" and focus your energy on being less miserable. Turn on the radio and jam out, call a friend, talk to the Lord, listen to an audiobook or podcast. Do whatever makes you happier and takes your mind off of the horrible traffic. It's inevitable—unfortunate things are going to happen, but keep in mind:

We are disturbed not by what happens to us, but by our thoughts about what happens to us.

Marie Forleo, web TV host and trainer in personal development refers to this concept as "making 'is-ness' your business" or in other words, get more interested in your reality or what is rather than complaining or wishing things would be different. We should engage our lives with enthusiasm.

How much better would your life be if you were constantly focused on the things you could control and no longer held hostage by your circumstances or victimized by the world?

My coach constantly preached to us about controlling the

"controllables." She would always say that in life, there are only two things we can control: our effort and our attitude. We had no control over the weather or field conditions, the calls the umpire made, the crowd. Just like elite athletes, focus on the things you can do something about and stop worrying about the things that are outside of your control. We are all human; we only have so much time and energy, and focusing on things outside of our control is a complete waste of it.

In life, we can't always control what happens to us, but we can control how we react to it.

Steven Covey, author of *The 7 Habits of Highly Effective People* (a MUST read), refers to it as Circle of Concern vs. Circle of Influence. Your Circle of Concern includes a range of things we worry about that aren't in our control—the past, our employees' behavior, the job market, the political climate, growing older, the opinions of others, etc. Our Circle of Influence only focuses on things we have control over and can do something about—our attitude, effort, preparation, diet, emotions, body language, etc. Utility players focus on things inside their Circle of Influence; they work on the things that they can do something about with an attitude that is positive, enlarging and magnifying. As utility players spend more of their time on the things they can control and less time on the things they can't, their Circle of Influence increases, and their Circle of Concern gets smaller and smaller.

What are some things in your life that deserve your time, energy, focus and attention? The things you're responsible for, the things you can control, things you can do something about? Focus on those things in order to be the best YOU!

Thinking back to my least favorite subject in school (science), I barely remember learning about how "nature abhors a vacuum." According to the ancient philosopher Aristotle, he concluded that nature requires every space to be filled with something, even if that something is invisible, colorless and odorless air. Just looking at our daily experiences with nature, we see how nature doesn't like a vacuum; or empty space. For instance, if you had a container and punctured a hole in it (creating a vacuum), nature would fill it pretty quickly with air. Where am I going here? Well, back when I was talking to one of my mentors, wondering what the heck I was going to do next with my life, not loving the job I was working, and not seeing doors for other opportunities opening up, he said, "Marti, nature is a vacuum." What the heck does that have to do with my life? I thought. Then he said, "Everywhere you go, there's a vacuum where someone's not fulfilling a responsibility, and you can step in and make something happen. Quit looking for a job. Use your unique ability—the things you do better than anyone else. Find the opportunity and fill the vacuum."

He was right. But how do we do this?

Figure out one or two things that you do better than everyone else.

Discover what your value is and focus on those things, and let someone else do the other stuff. It's important to take inventory of your talents and capabilities, then you'll figure out what you can uniquely offer, and plan ways and means of giving others advantages, services, strategies, and ideas that you believe you can successfully deliver.

Forget about "a job."

I learned this is the timeless book, *Think and Grow Rich* by Napoleon Hill. Forget whether or not there is an opening or if they're hiring.

Forget the usual routine of "do you have room for me?" and concentrate on what you can give.

Remember, it's a process.

It's not an end all, be all; you can constantly take inventory of your abilities and add new skills, grow and cultivate your current specialties, and become an essential asset to others. Find what your unique abilities are and develop them like crazy. The better you get at a skill, the more satisfaction you'll get from that skill. So ask yourself, what do I want to specialize in? What can I offer? What value can I bring to the table? Focus on what you can do for others and there will always be space for you.

As a utility player, you can be flexible in opportunities when you step out of your comfort zone, focus on the things you can control, and concentrate on what you can give to others. You'll also be able to create opportunities in your life regardless of your circumstances or what life throws at you.

UTILITY WORKOUTS

DAILY CHALLENGE

For the next week, do something every day that makes you challenge yourself to step out of your comfort zone. On your calendar, each day, write the one thing you will do that day to challenge yourself. It can be as simple as saying hello to a stranger or starting a conversation with a random person, or something more elaborate like taking a dance or cooking class. Do something that kind of scares you. For example, I'm afraid of heights and the deep blue sea, so I could decide to go cliff jumping to face my fears. Track your progress and how you feel after your daily challenge. The more you practice stepping out of your comfort zone, the easier it gets.

BUILD YOUR EXPERIENCE

Do a career industry search on LinkedIn or Google. Highlight the industry categories that sound remotely interesting to you. Once you have a list of 5 - 10 industries, then research the top businesses in your area within those industries. Once you have a list of 20 businesses, call and ask if you can come by and shadow them for a day, or volunteer for a week to learn more about their company. This will help you gain experience, and learn to be flexible and create your own opportunities.

CONTROL THE CONTROLLABLES

Draw a line down the middle of your paper and on one side, write "Circle of Influence" and on the other side of the line write "Circle of Concern." Take 60 seconds to write down all the things you can think of in your Circle of Influence (things you can control) and then list the things in your Circle of Concern (things outside of your control). This week, only focus on the things that are listed in your "Circle of Influence" and notice how this makes you feel.

CHAPTER 6

Stamina in Creating Habits

I am in no way exempt from the words you're about to read. This is probably one of the biggest lessons that I had to learn and am still learning this very moment in my life. Okay so, ain't it crazy how many ads, commercials, and billboards come bombarding our TVs, inboxes and daily commutes right after the first of the year about diet or weight loss programs, get-rich quick offers, or the newest lotion/potions, Vitamix products that will change your life overnight with three easy payments? It's hard not to be tempted by these "opportunities" that all sound too good to be true. But I know, the hardest part when you set a goal or make up your mind to achieve something is realizing that it won't happen right away.

SUCCESS IS NOT A SPRINT, IT'S A MARATHON!

Utility players have stamina in creating habits. Success doesn't happen overnight; you won't get fit in a week, and your life won't change unless you make changes and commit to them. YOU MUST PUT IN THE WORK — again and again — or it's not going to happen.

I'm sure you've heard the saying "success is not a sprint, it's a marathon," but after reading *The Compound Effect* by Darren Hardy, I truly began to internalize the idea that it's not about doing a thousand things right. It's about doing a few things right a thousand times.

Imagine someone who drinks soda all of the time, then decides to replace soda with water. After one week, this person probably won't see much of a change, but by staying consistent for the next year, the results would be remarkable! I'm telling you, over the past year I've learned that the little things we do consistently on a daily basis will add up over time into the big things. One of the biggest leadership experts of our time, John C. Maxwell, said, **"You will never change your life until you change something you do daily. The secret of your success is found in your daily routine."**

Everyone has habits and routines that they've developed over time—some good, some bad, some healthy, some unhealthy, some conscious, some unconscious. We all have them. What are the habits and routines in your life that are helping you reach your goals? What are the ones that are holding you back?

In 2008, Michael Phelps was swimming in the butterfly race at the Olympics. Halfway through the race his goggles got filled up with water. He couldn't see a thing. Not only did he go on to win the race, he set a new world record — literally with his eyes closed! I love telling this story to athletes and students, I always ask them how they think he was able to do that? They yell out things like "Determination!" "Grit!" "Perseverance!" All great answers. But the true reason is, habits. Michael Phelps had put in the work and practiced that race so many times that it became habit. It became second-nature. He didn't even need to see where he was going, he could swim literally with his eyes closed and still succeed.

Successful people are no different than you and me. Success isn't something reserved for inherently talented, special individuals and it doesn't happen from doing one huge gigantic thing right. Successful people are ordinary individuals that make a decision to put in the work, doing small things right, consistently, on a daily basis. They succeed on purpose! You can have the best goals and the best intentions in the world, but those alone will not get you to your destination. It's your daily habits, choices and influences that bring you momentum and allow you to accelerate to where you want to go.

Author Darren Hardy says, "Some of our best intentions fail because we don't have a system of execution." As athletes and former athletes, we know the importance of having a daily routine. We're used to going to practice and putting in the work even when we don't feel like doing it. This type of work ethic doesn't change when you leave the playing field.

> **EXCELLENCE IS NOT AN ACT, BUT A HABIT!**

Think about three areas in your life where you're least consistent, and then think of six key behaviors relevant to your goals. What new habits would you like to add to your daily routine that will help you reach your goals? When you get down to the nitty-gritty, your new attitudes and behaviors need to be incorporated into your monthly, weekly and daily routines to impact any real, positive change. And eventually, like brushing your teeth or washing your hands (assuming everyone exercises these good habits), it becomes unconscious routine.

Like Aristotle says, **"We are what we repeatedly do. Excellence, then, is not an act, but a habit."**

Lately I've been immersed in the Netflix Docuseries, Last Chance U, which is about a win-at-all-cost football program at East Mississippi Community College. They recruit several talented athletes who got kicked out of D1 schools after making bad personal decisions. Essentially, this football program gives them another chance to prove themselves and make their football dreams come true. There are so many reasons why this documentary has me hooked and I won't go into all of them right now, but on one episode, the coach made a comment that stuck in my head: Excellence is not an accident.

Did you catch that? Excellence is not an accident, and, I would add, neither is failure. Your intention, effort, and execution lead to your results. It's about choice, not chance.

All of the athletes in this docuseries make bad decisions off the football field. There's a recurring theme in this series; a faulty belief that I have seen other athletes have as I have traveled the country speaking. I have found that sometimes athletes believe that their talent (and that alone) is going to give them the respect and opportunities they need to be successful. I have to remind them that you earn respect off the field as well. Talent alone isn't enough. What you do matters. The choices you make on a daily basis matter. You always have a choice. There's a podcast that offers an intense example of this. It's called Gladiator and it's all about the Aaron Hernandez story.

> **CHOICE IS AT THE CENTER OF ALL SUCCESS AND FAILURE. IT IS WHAT WE CHOOSE THAT MAKES THE BIGGEST DIFFERENCE.**

This is a vivid example of how terrible choices off the field led to devastating results all-around.

We can choose to blame circumstances outside of our control for the outcomes we experience. But at the end of the day, we are solely responsible for the choices we make and the eventual outcome. Too often we sleepwalk through our choices. We default to choices that our society and culture tell us we should make. Often, we end up choosing what appears easy instead of hard, only to find out that the hard choice ends up being the right one. I remind my audiences, and I'm telling you: you have the power to decide what you want to do. The right thing to do is not easy—it usually comes with hardships and challenges, against certain odds, and at times contrary to popular opinion or common thinking. But it is in those choices that greatness is found. I've said it once and I'll say it again—it's your daily habits, choices and influences that bring you momentum and allow you to accelerate to where you want to go.

We each have the power and freedom to choose right from wrong. Greatness is not served on a silver platter; it is earned by the choices we make against all odds with the will, determination and perseverance to succeed. Always remember that you can change your life simply by making better choices. It is up to you. You can make better lifestyle decisions, get rid of old habits, change unwanted situations, choose a better diet, better friends, have better reactions to situations and challenges, etc. Start with the wisdom, integrity and will to make the right choices for you, and you'll have the courage to achieve great things.

ONE SIMPLE HABIT THAT CAN CHANGE YOUR LIFE

I remember it like it was yesterday. I was about 7 or 8 years old, waking up to the sound of my mom yelling from downstairs, "breakfast is ready!" As soon as she said it, I started to smell the eggs, grits, toast, and turkey bacon she had been cooking. I hopped out of my bed and hurried down the stairs to try and beat my brother and sister to the table. My dad was last to come downstairs and even before he sat down, before I could even take my first bite, I heard him say sternly, "Marti! I know you are not about to take a bite out of that food without your bed being made! Get back up those stairs right now and MAKE YOUR BED!" I dropped the fork and ran back upstairs to make my bed.

My dad is not a military man, but by the way he ran his household, you would think otherwise. In my home we were washing dishes as soon as we were tall enough to reach the sink, and doing laundry as soon as we were old enough to say the word "clothes." Making our beds in the morning was a requirement before we could do anything else. And for the longest time, I didn't understand why. I thought it was just my dad trying to keep his house in order while annoying me at the same time. I would complain to myself and rationalize thoughts in my head like, "Why make up the bed if I'm going to get back in it later?" "What a waste of time!" "I don't have time for this." "Who cares? No one is going to see it but me, so who cares?"

In spite of my lazy-mindset, I continued to make my bed every morning and it became an unconscious habit that I carried with me through college, and even now. I never leave my house or even start my day if my bed is not made. It is the first thing I do in the morning, even if I'm running late.

Why is making your bed such a big deal? Besides the obvious reasons of how it makes your room look ten times better, cleaner and tidier, can this one 3-minute task really make that much of a difference in your life? The answer is YES! It's the first finished task of the day that you can check off your list! I like to start my day off with a win right away, and although it may be minor, you can feel a small sense of accomplishment when you make your own bed.

Making your bed can help start you off feeling confident every morning and affect your self-esteem throughout the day. It will encourage you to finish another task, then another, and so on — increasing your productivity! In the book *The Power of Habit*, author Charles Duhigg describes the simple act of making your bed as a keystone habit (like cooking your own food or exercising), which is essentially a minor feel-good habit that serves as a catalyst for other good habits.

According to research from the National Sleep Foundation and a survey of 2,000 Americans conducted by market research company OnePoll and commissioned by sleep research site Sleepopolis, 60% of people don't make their beds, 28% do, and 12% pay a housekeeper to make it for them. But get this—71% of the bed-makers consider themselves happy, while 62% of the non-bed-makers admit to being unhappy. Bed-makers were also more likely to enjoy their jobs, own a home, exercise regularly and feel well-rested while the non-bed-makers were more likely to hate their jobs, rent apartments, avoid the gym and wake up tired. All you non-bed-makers out there, calm down. I'm not saying that you can't be happy or successful because you'd rather have rumpled sheets. That is far from the truth! These factors are not causation, just correlation. But it's the little things in life that matter most, for they add up to the big things. So if you'd like to live a happier life, be more productive and develop better habits that will increase your success, start with making your bed every morning and go from there.

UTILITY WORKOUTS

IDENTIFY YOUR HABITS

In order to develop good habits, you must be aware of our current habits. Take inventory of the things you are constantly doing or seeing in your life. For example, if you are constantly finding yourself broke and financially struggling, chances are you have a bad habit of spending more than you earn. Write down 5 of your habits that you love, 5 habits that you want to get rid of, and 5 habits that you would like to gain.

IDENTIFY YOUR TRIGGERS

In order to get rid of the habits you no longer want, you have to understand your triggers and obstacles. We all need support or release for our frustrations in moments of weakness and vulnerability. Reaching for alcohol, drugs, over-eating, or other unhealthy habits is not the answer. If something unfortunate happens, which will happen eventually, you have to find a healthy alternative to dealing with it. Next to your bad habits, write down your triggers and brainstorm some healthier alternatives to dealing with these obstacles.

CREATE NEW POSITIVE HABITS

Focus on one habit at a time and devise a plan. Take one of the 5 habits you identified that you wanted to have and focus on it for the next 5 weeks. During this time, focus on developing this habit using visualizations (spending focused time on seeing the image of yourself doing it right and getting your desired outcomes) and affirmations (speaking positively to yourself about achieving your new habits) to help. It helps to have an accountability group or person to help you stick to your plan. Let your accountability group know what you're trying to accomplish and enlist their support. They will help keep you from falling back into old habits/routines that you're trying to shake off. And lastly, find healthy ways to reward yourself for successfully implementing your new good habit throughout the week.

MAKE YOUR BED

This utility workout is that simple—for the next 30 days, make your bed every day, even if you don't plan on leaving the house. Make your bed first thing in the morning after you get out of it. See how this makes you feel after 30 days and let it turn into a keystone habit!

CHAPTER 7

Sportsmanship in Life

In life, we were all born as takers. When we were babies, everything was "mine." We wore bibs, and we were used to being fed and getting the things that we wanted. But at some point in life, we realized it was time to strip that bib from our necks and lose that self-centered mindset of "Me! Me! Me!" We come to understand that we should drape a napkin over our arm, like a butler, and go through life with a mindset of "how may I serve you?" Instead of always asking ourselves what someone can do for us, or what's in this for you, we should start asking ourselves what we can do for others. The late great motivation guru Zig Ziglar said it best:

You can have everything in life you want if you will just help enough other people get what they want.

Utility players apply the principles of sportsmanship. When I was competing in softball at UCLA, one of our guiding principles was "Team Over Self." This meant that no one person on the team was more important than the team as a whole. We all shared the same goal and vision—to win a National Championship. We knew this wouldn't be possible unless we worked together and always chose the team over our personal needs. It was a completely selfless mindset, and competing on a team with others that cared about me just as much as I cared about them was a life-changing experience. We ended up winning the NCAA title in 2010, and this was only possible because we came together, trusted each other and competed with a "Team Over Self" mentality. Considering others and playing for something bigger than myself was a powerful life lesson that I will never forget.

Think about your visions, plans and goals and ask yourself why you'd like to achieve these things in the first place? Is your motivating force characterized by what you can get versus what you can give? Were your visions, plans and goals created based on the needs of others and derived from a genuine belief that you can help other people get what they want? Most people do not frame their goals with this mindset, so don't feel bad if helping others get what they want was not your intention.

Today I want you to rethink your intentions. The moment you shift from "self-centered" intentions to "others-centered" intentions, you will unlock your potential and change your life while changing other's lives as well. If your motives are mostly self-centered, your value is diminished and your sincerity will be questioned.

We often have self-limiting beliefs that hold us back from giving ourselves (our money, time, energy) to others. When we resist giving freely, we send messages to our mind that say "there isn't enough," "I won't get any more," "I feel safer with this in my pocket," "I might need this for an emergency," or "I can't trust other people to do the right thing." All of these limiting factors hold us back from being of service to others.

But in fact, the more you hold on to your limited thinking, the harder it will be to attract the things you want in life. Want to receive more? Then give more. It's that simple.

If you want to get love you have to give love; if you want to get respect you have to give respect; if you want to get help, you have to give help. Renowned author and business consultant, Dan Kennedy said, "The window you receive from is made bigger by the window you give through." He also agrees that one of the biggest secrets to wealth is giving. Give freely without expecting anything in return. Give your all; give massive value in everything you do. Know that there is always room to give and trust that there will always be more flowing in. The best way to find yourself is to lose yourself in the service of others (Gandhi said it), so choose an "others centered" rather than "self-centered" mindset. Serve others first before you serve yourself and watch how your life changes. Watch how much more of an impact you make on the world you live in. Take basketball for example. Have you ever played on a team or seen a team play with ball-hogs—players that never pass the ball, always take the shot and try to do it all on their own? It's extremely difficult for the team to succeed with players that are ball-hogs. Brian Skinner, a researcher at the University of Minnesota, discovered that teams that share the ball and pass more end up scoring more, and are much more efficient as a whole. It's the same in life. You have to share with others. Don't be a ball-hog—pass the ball more!

> **SPORTSMANSHIP HAS A LOT TO DO WITH HUMILITY.**

Sportsmanship has a lot to do with humility. When you are humble, you are able to recognize your own shortcomings and limitations. As a utility player, it's important to put your pride aside and have the confidence to surrender your need for the attention, and instead, let others enjoy the glory.

Consider this moral tale written by M. Peer Mohamed Sardhar that taught me a great life lesson.

There was a learned scientist who mastered a formula of reproducing himself. He did it so perfectly that it was almost impossible to tell the reproduction from the original. One day he was doing research and he realized the Angel of Death was searching for him. In order to remain immortal, he reproduced a dozen copies of himself and when the Angel of Death knocked on his door, the Angel of Death was at a loss to know which of the thirteen before him was the original scientist. The Angel of Death left confused, until he thought of a clever idea. He showed up again and addressed all 13 scientists, "Sir, you must be a genius to have succeeded in making such a perfect reproduction formula for yourself, but I have discovered a flaw in your work, just one tiny little flaw." In that moment the original scientist immediately jumped out and shouted, "That's impossible in my work! Small flaw?! What flaw?" "Right here" said the Angel as he picked up the scientist from among the replicas and carried him off.

Pride is an attitude in all of us that can cause the most devastating consequences in both personal and professional life. A proud or arrogant person has a swollen ego, or thinks they're better or more deserving than others. The root cause of pride is self-centeredness. As a former athlete who was a part of a very successful program, I admit that it got hard to monitor my pride and ego. Growing up in sports and experiencing great moments of pride from winning championships, or hearing crowds chant my name, or having fans asking for autographs can make it harder to keep your ego in check. I had to constantly remind myself that my ability and success on the field came from the help of others—great teammates, coaches and support systems that had my back. Knowledge and skill can take you to the top, but just like the scientist in the story who could not control his pride and lost his life, ego can pull you down immediately. It is the enemy of happiness and success.

Deep down we want everyone else to meet all of our needs, desires, and expectations, and we often act as if our needs are more important than those of others. It's time to have a gut-check. Check your ego, Amigo! Don't forget that there is only One that is the ultimate authority and in control of the Universe, and He is Almighty God. We have to replace pride and ego with humility. True humility begins with a heartfelt belief that others have made it possible for you to have everything valuable in your life. If you believe this, you'll start to carry yourself with the eager and grateful spirit of a learner; one who welcomes and values the input and contributions of others.

In sports, the teams with the most humility are usually more successful. When you have a team full of talented players, humility is a secret ingredient that will help that team work better together in the midst of multiple superstars. Appreciating others strengths, giving credit where credit is due, and highlighting the team or organization's success over individual achievements are great ways to build humility and sportsmanship. When you can admit that you don't have all of the answers and you are willing and open to learn from others, you are practicing humility and helping the team grow. You are being a utility player and applying sportsmanship in life.

We all play leadership roles, no matter how big or small, and our behavior is contagious. I talk to coaches often about the importance of creating a positive atmosphere to improve the culture and performance of the team. What type of environment are you bringing to your team based on your behavior? The way you act as a leader of your team has influence on the emotion and behavior of everyone else. It affects the team's performance. Focus on having a positive attitude and making humility a core practice of your team. Humility reflects how close your team gets to their potential and how long they will stay there. When your athletes are driven by things bigger than just personal success, the opportunity of team success is much higher. This type of environment will help athletes go on to be positive role models and have sportsmanship in life beyond the playing field.

In order to exhibit sportsmanship in your life outside of sports, you have to be willing to consider others and know when to let others lead. Often times, people believe more the solutions that they themselves have discovered than the solutions presented to them. In other words, people will understand an idea/solution/plan/concept more if they believe they thought of it, rather than someone else telling them what to do. That is why it is so important to be interested rather than just interesting. When building relationships and connections, ask questions more. Help people discover their own truths rather than blabbing out yours.

It's important to let people discover their truths in the workplace as well. As a "salesperson," or better put, a deliverer of ideas, strategies and impact, I am constantly addressing and serving the needs of others. I'm always looking for ways to make organizations better. In order for new clients to jump on board, it's my job to communicate our company's features and benefits, while helping new clients discover that we are a solution to their needs. I could choose to go into an initial meeting and tell people that they are doing things wrong and they should be working with us, but no matter how true or false that may be, it will not go over well. Instead, I have to ask the right questions and help them discover for themselves that we are the solution to their needs.

I remember my mom telling me that I'd better put a jacket on before going outside or else I would freeze. Instantly I would respond with, "I don't need a jacket." Then I would go outside and freeze. But because she told me to put on a jacket rather than me deciding for myself, even though I was cold, I wouldn't go back inside to get my jacket. Don't judge me, I know it's petty, but I know I ain't the only one that does this. I know some of you are guilty of this stuff too!

As you can see, this concept goes beyond the workplace. You can use the concept of discovery to make your personal relationships more effective by trying these strategies:

LISTEN TO UNDERSTAND INSTEAD OF LISTENING TO RESPOND. Have you ever been in a disagreement with someone and that someone cuts you off to make a point before you finish your thought? That's because in conversations, we often don't listen to understand, we listen to respond. Always let someone finish their statement and listen to what they are saying. Put yourself in their shoes and try to understand it from their point of view before you respond.

BE MORE INTERESTED THAN INTERESTING. Have you ever been talking to a friend, telling them a story about something that happened to you, and immediately the friend starts talking about how that relates to her, or she starts telling an even bigger story about the time something similar happened to her? Sometimes you don't even get to finish your story before a friend starts blabbing on and on about themselves. Don't be that person! You don't need to match someone else's story. It's not a competition. Try to do the opposite and be interested instead of just interesting.

ASK, DON'T TELL. I remember when I was going through a tough time on the playing field, in a slump, and not getting the results I wanted. My teammate pulled me aside and asked, "What are your goals when you go into each game?" My response was, "My goal is to get at least one hit every game." But I was getting so frustrated because I hadn't gotten a hit in the past two games and was falling into a slump. She then said to me, "I understand your frustration. When you go up to bat, can you control whether or not you get a hit?" I responded, "Not really." Then she asked me, "What are some things you can control when you're at the plate?" I said, "Swinging at good pitches. Being on time and hitting the ball hard." She asked me, "What if you shifted your mindset and focused on those things you can control instead of getting a hit?" I then immediately decided to change my goal to swinging at good pitches and hitting the ball hard every at bat, not worrying whether or not I got a hit, and my results got a whole lot better. This was thanks to my teammate who asked me great questions and helped me discover the answers I needed. When a friend comes to you to chat about something going on in his/her life, instead of lecturing them on what you believe is the right solution, ask questions. If you help them discover the solution rather than delivering one to them, it will stick better because the idea is "theirs" and not yours.

UTILITY WORKOUTS

CHECK YOUR EGO, AMIGO

Make a list of the things you value or the things that are good in your life. Here is my list:

- Relationship with God
- My family
- My family's health
- My health
- My friends
- My mentors
- My career

Next to each thing of value, write the names of the people who have helped you in that area of your life. Your spirit of gratefulness will rise, you'll become more attentive and you will start to focus more on the needs of others rather than personal ego.

GIVE A COMPLIMENT

When you are going about your day, make a conscious effort to give a genuine compliment to the people you come across. Before starting a conversation, let them know something positive about themselves or something they did that you appreciate. Practice giving out compliments like candy!

RELATIONSHIPS BUILT ON SPORTSMANSHIP

Applying sportsmanship principles in all of your life means you have relationships that are win-win: both parties feel a mutual benefit from the relationship. If you could design your own script for a great relationship, what benefits would you want to offer other people? What benefits would you like others to offer you?

PART 3 — UTILITY TRAINING AND POSITIONING

A strong utility player, when fully developed, has immense value to a team. In part 2, we laid down the foundation as we discovered the common values of utility players—strength of character, flexibility in opportunity, stamina in creating habits, and sportsmanship in life. We will now explore all of life's positions that a utility player fulfills, showing how to maximize each of those roles while maintaining a culture of excellence.

PART 3

UTILITY TRAINING AND POSITIONING

CHAPTER 8

Be a Good Teammate

I started playing organized sports at 7 years old. Before that, I would never speak to anyone. I was so shy, I had to have my brother who is a year and a half older than me walk up to other little kids on the playground to ask them if they wanted to play with me. I would see another little girl playing handball and I would go find my big brother and point to her, he would grab my hand and walk me over and do all of the talking for me, "Hi! What's your name?" he would ask on my behalf. "Nice to meet you. This is my sister, Marti. She really loves playing handball, and I see you like to play handball too. Marti is really good; can she play with you?" And they would say yes, and he would leave and I would start to play, still not saying a word. I was so afraid to speak, I'm not sure why but the thought of something stupid coming out of my mouth terrified me so I'd rather just listen to others and watch. I was a huge introvert, which led me to get picked on and bullied by other kids, especially when my big brother wasn't around. It wasn't until my parents signed me up to play organized sports, I started to find my voice. I started to learn how to communicate (because I had to out on the field). I started to make my own friends naturally, thanks to sports. As athletes, many of us have met some of our best friends out on the playing field. Sports have brought us together and helped us build relationships.

When I played softball at UCLA, I considered our team a family. This meant that no matter what happened, we would have each other's backs, respect each other, and support one another. Not all of us were best friends with each other, but we definitely loved one another and would go to war for our teammates. That's what a family does — supports you on good and bad days.

What does it take to be a top utility player as it relates to your position as a family member or a true friend?

IT TAKES ENGAGEMENT, IT TAKES CONNECTION AND IT TAKES GRATITUDE

At UCLA, our team success had a lot to do with our focus and engagement on a unified mission (to win a national championship), our connection with one another, and showing each other appreciation and gratitude. Being fully engaged means you are present and involved in the pursuit of a common goal. When you are engaged with someone or something, it has your attention, support and concern. You truly care about that person or thing. When you are engaged in something you show up, you're willing to take risks, and your support is unconditional and not dependent on what you get in return. It's authentic.

When it comes to family, a utility player is engaged and involved and has the desire to be an intricate member of the family. On our team at UCLA, we knew what each other's goals were on and off of the field. We were involved in each other's lives and supported each other. We would often share our goals before practice and what areas we were looking to grow in on that particular day. Then we'd hold each other accountable and help each other reach those goals.

In sports, you have to know how to be a great teammate. If you know how to be a great teammate on the playing field, then that can translate off of the field and help you be a great friend in life. You have to be dependable and reliable out on the playing field. There's an African proverb/philosophy called "ubuntu" which means, "I am what I am because of who we all are." This means I can't be all I can be until you are all you can be; no one person's goals are more important than the entirety of the team. We had a team-over-self mentality, at UCLA which means we supported each other on good and bad days. We put the team's interests above our own, which meant at times we had to sacrifice our individual happiness or satisfaction for the greater good of our team. If you are a true friend, you are willing to sacrifice your individual comfort or satisfaction for someone else's.

A GREAT TEAMMATE ENCOURAGES OTHERS.

Connection is also key in building relationships. Connection involves finding common ground, building rapport and communicating in a way that others can receive. At UCLA, we were able to connect as a team by understanding that everyone had her own leadership role. Once we owned our role, we were able to impact and inspire action. Everyone on the team was a leader in her own way. There were vocal leaders, competitive leaders, spiritual leaders, social leaders, intuitive leaders, emotional leaders, academic leaders, community leaders, etc. When you're on a team, it's important to understand that leadership isn't all about talent or skill level; being a great leader is about making those around you better. Once you understand your leadership style and how others lead, it helps the team adapt and relate to each other more effectively. This ultimately allows teammates to have greater impact and inspire action.

One of the responsibilities of a great teammate in life is to encourage. Encouragement creates hope —the power that gives a person the confidence to step out and try. Encouragement fuels confidence, positive thinking and attitude. When you can encourage your friends, you can stimulate their minds, influence their perspectives and keep them from giving up. Encouragement gives them strength in their weakness and faith that anything is possible in spite of the current circumstances. The kind of encouragement I'm talking about can be very simple; it can come from a single principle or phrase. The positive results that come from believing the encouragement can give your friends the hope needed to recognize opportunities and seize the day.

It is often said that at the end of your life, it's not where you've gone, what you did or what you have; it's who you have beside you that matters most. Relationships are the most important thing that you can build. Sylvester McNutt said it best, "we live in a generation that is highly skilled at allowing connections to fade away. Because of social media and cell phones, we think people are replaceable, and that's silly. You cannot replace the energy of someone who is genuine especially if they're putting consistent effort out, to be in your life. Appreciate them, cherish them, those people are gold."

Cherishing someone means valuing them enough to seek to understand them. We often get so focused on changing someone.

Our selfish inclination is to try and make others more like us. Instead, we should work to do the unnatural and uncommon thing: accept people for who they are and try to understand where they're coming from. Once you can truly accept others for who they are, and seek to understand, your relationship will grow to greater heights together.

THE LOVE LANGUAGES

The essential factors of strong relationships are those small, little things that seem insignificant but mean so much to someone else. *The 5 Love Languages* by Gary Chapman is one of my favorite books about building relationships. It's not just about love or romantic relationships; it's also about strengthening friendships and general relationships. The idea is everyone has a language (i.e. quality time, acts of service, gifts, words of affirmation and physical touch) that they speak when it comes to love and feeling loved by others. One of the basic core needs of humanity is to feel loved by others, so it's important to understand how someone receives love so you can love them in their language. We all know the golden rule: treat others how you want to be treated. But there's a better rule—the platinum rule. Treat others how they want to be treated. If you can show others love in their language, it will help you understand people better and build relationships. I highly recommend reading the book and taking the test to discover your love language and recognize the love languages others have.

GRATITUDE

Another important quality of a great teammate and in relationships is gratitude. When it comes to family and true friends, showing your appreciation is a great way to build the relationship. Utility players practice gratitude. They realize that anywhere they get, they didn't get there alone. It takes the support and prayers around you to keep you covered and moving forward.

Everyone wants to be appreciated. It doesn't matter how rich or famous you are, we all want to be valued and know we're important. Expressing gratitude and appreciation only takes a moment; it doesn't have to be this long drawn-out immaculate display. Sometimes, all it takes is a quick phone call, a short note, or one simple sentence to make someone's day and show your appreciation. Utility players understand that thoughts of gratitude, graciousness, thankfulness and appreciation are free. Begin with your family and true friends. Make it a habit to express appreciation to your people often. Sow words of love lavishly, consistently and to every person who is worthy. Developing a passion for gratitude, thankfulness and appreciation is a characteristic of extraordinary and uncommon people—utility players.

UTILITY WORKOUTS

CONSISTENT COMMUNICATION

The best way to stay engaged with your teammates (family and true friends) is to communicate consistently. Reaching out to a family member or friend weekly and asking these simple questions go a long way: How are you? What's new? How can I help?

When you are in the know and care about what is going on in

your people's life, then you can be better equipped to offer your help or connect them to the things they need. For instance, if a family member tells me that they are very interested in film and TV, and I meet someone that's in that industry, I will introduce them. Another example is my dad loves chocolate, and so I will often bring him his favorite chocolates just to show him I care and make him happy. It's the thought that counts. Know what your teammates are interested in, stay engaged, and make those connections.

GRATITUDE LETTERS

Practice gratitude. There is always something to be grateful for. For the next 30 days, write a short thank you to a different member of your family, friend, or teammate every day to tell them how much you appreciate them. Thirty notes in 30 days. Expressing gratitude to your teammates will result in positive emotions while also building a relationship.

THE LOVE LANGUAGE TEST

What is your love language and the language of your teammates? Take the assessment with your friends and family. Find out what their love language is so you can love them in the way they want to receive it! www.5lovelanguages.com. Also, read the book *The 5 Love Languages* by Gary Chapman. You won't be disappointed.

BE MORE INTERESTED THAN INTERESTING

Do you consider yourself a good listener? Why or why not? What prevents you from listening more closely to those you care about? Try a 24-hour media fast. No TV, no Facebook, no Instagram, no radio, no computer, no social media. Try to tune out all of your distractions and be present in the moment. Listen to the people in your life. After the media fast, write down how it affected you.

ONE MONTH TO LIVE

If you only had one month left to live, who would you want to spend that time with? Who would you need to apologize to? What friend(s) in your life need to be reminded today that you love them and care about them? What is stopping you (if anything) from taking the time to say these words now?

Choose one person in your life that you know you have hurt with your words, actions, or silence. Hand-write a letter asking for this person's forgiveness and explain all that you'd like to say before it's too late. Put the letter away for a few days, then revisit it to decide whether or not you want to send it. That decision is up to you.

MAKE SOME TIME

Take a look at your schedule over the next few days. No matter how busy you are, find a time to surprise someone you love. You can take a friend to a favorite restaurant or show up to work with donuts or coffee. Whatever you decide, just find a way to add quality connections to your life on a daily basis.

TOP FIVE

What are the top 5 most important relationships in your life? Diagnose and jot down what you believe each important relationship in your life needs in order to be healthier and stronger. It could be as simple as spending more time together, discussing an unsettled issue, or sending someone a note or email just to say you're thinking about them.

CHAPTER

Be a Student

As a student, we go to class, study and do homework in order to prepare for the test. And it's the same in sports — we practice and prepare, and we put our practice to work on game day (the test). Playing sports in school is not an easy thing to balance. It's important to remember while in school and participating in sports, we are students first, then athletes—that's why it's called "student-athlete." But even when you leave the playing field, it's important not to neglect the position of student. Even after you graduate and your days of sitting in class are over, you should still be a student in life — remaining curious, open-minded and willing to learn new ways to expand your scope. The moment you think you know everything is the moment that you lose in what life has to offer.

As a utility player, the position of student means you're constantly learning and growing. There are lessons all around you and you can learn from just about anyone. Most people can learn the basics of things fairly quickly, but the sad part is most people peak at a level of proficiency that they are satisfied with. Once they get good enough at a level that makes them happy, they stop there. A very small percentage of people never peak —they keep learning, growing and improving for years. Those are the ones that separate themselves from the rest of the pack; those are the people that go on to reach unique success. Those are the ultimate utility players.

When I was in grade school, I knew at a young age that I wanted to be at the top of my class and get good grades. It was something that my parents valued, and all the other authorities in my life valued, so quite naturally, I valued it as well. My competitive spirit allowed me to work hard in the classroom just like I did on the softball field. I knew I wasn't the smartest person in the class, but I didn't want that ever to be an excuse to why I wasn't able to perform at a high level.

My father also instilled a work ethic in me by not handing things to me or making things easy. I remember countless times I would be at home doing my homework and I would ask my dad, "Hey dad, what does this word mean?" and instead of telling me the answer, he would hand me a dictionary and make me look the word up for myself. I remember I would get so mad and think to myself, "Ugh!! Why doesn't he just tell me! He already knows the answer; why do I have to look it up?!" Making me look up words, and showing me how to find the answers for myself was one of the best things my dad did for me. He taught me how to put in the work and not expect things to be easy. At a young age, I understood that my results in the classroom were a matter of choice, not circumstance. I knew that if I tried hard and put in the work, I would get the results.

I remember the moment I realized that my brain didn't move as fast as others'. I was in the second grade and up until then, I thought I was a genius. I thought I was the smartest kid in the class. I remember I thought I should be moved up a grade because I was smarter than everyone else. In the second grade, I started to notice other people finishing their reading faster than me, or others finding the answer more quickly. One kid in my class in particular was a kid-genius. He was that kid that seemed to always know the answer without having to think too hard or look it up in the dictionary. He was so smart; I remember I would go home from school and practice my time tables, reading faster, and spelling correctly just to go back to school the next day in order to keep up with him. I knew he was "stronger, faster, better" but I didn't let that discourage me. Instead, I worked harder. The biggest lesson I learned as a student was determination and hard work can outlast talent. Getting good grades or finishing at the top of your class is a decision that you can make.

STAY ATTENTIVE

Another way to remain a student in life is to stay attentive. Be present in the things you're working on. Eliminate distractions. Not everyone learns the same way or at the same pace. Get to know your learning style; it will help set you up for success. In high school I had a 4.13 GPA and was able to get into Ivy League schools with my extracurricular activities. At UCLA, I graduated with a 3.49 GPA. It wasn't by chance that these were my results, I worked my tail off and I knew what I needed to do so I could be successful.

In college, I would arrive to class early and sit in the first two rows because it was hard to be distracted by anything else going on in class when I was up front and could look the professor in the eye. This increased my chances of success. I would take a computer and record the lesson, all while taking hand-written notes because even though I was hearing it and recording it, writing it down helped my brain retain the information better. This allowed me to go back and listen to the information again if I didn't understand something. I would attend the professor's office hours with prepared questions on the lessons. Even though having a tutor wasn't required if your average was above a C, for my toughest classes, I used the tutors provided by the athletic department. I would sign up for tutoring because I always knew that my chances of succeeding in that class would increase if I had a tutor helping me as well.

I would often go to my tutor with a complex topic from class and say, "Can you explain this to me as if I were a child...like 5 years old?" I wanted to make it as simple as possible. Even if it was information I probably should have already known, I didn't get embarrassed for admitting I didn't know it or needed to be reminded. I tried to keep a growth mindset, which meant that my level of intelligence was not fixed; I could always grow and learn something with enough focus, proper tutors and practice.

Once I felt like I understood the information, I would go teach it to my friends who were struggling. Not only did I help them to understand it better, it also helped me learn and memorize the information. All these things set me up for a better opportunity to succeed in the classroom, and I use these techniques in life as well.

TIME MANAGEMENT

Another way I was able to succeed as a student is managing my time wisely. A great deal of your attention has to do with how you're managing your time, and a great way to set yourself up for success as a life-long student is being impeccable with how you spend your time. Imagine if you had an extra day in the week. A day between Sunday and Monday— let's call it Funday. Wouldn't that be nice to have an extra day? How would you spend your Funday? Getting more work done? Maybe spending more time with your family or close friends? Maybe going on a hike or trying out a new adventure or project you've always wanted to begin but never got around to?

Even though we don't have an extra day in the week, there is a way we can free-up more time in our lives to do the things we really care about. If we were to calculate the number of hours we're awake over the next year starting now, assuming we sleep an average of 7 hours a night, we'd be awake for 6,205 hours over the next 365 days. 6,205 hours! That's a lot of time to manage! But can we really manage our time?

We can manage money—we can make it, save it, spend it, and invest it. We can manage our money and tell it exactly where to go (we might not be great at this, but it is possible to do). We can also manage people — we direct people, reward people, ask people to do things and lead people. But what about time? Can we tell time to slow down? Move faster? Stop? No, we can't.

You can't actually manage time, but you can manage how you spend it! The challenge is not to manage time, but to manage ourselves and how we choose to invest it.

After reading *The 7 Habits of Highly Effective People* by Stephen Covey, I was introduced to the Time Matrix, and after understanding this time matrix and using it to my advantage, it increased my efficiency and achievement in ways I never could even imagine! At the top of the matrix you have things that are important, at the bottom you have the things that are unimportant, on the left side you have the things that are urgent and on the right side you have things that are non-urgent.

This time matrix will help you organize and execute your day around your priorities. If calendars and appointment books aren't your thing, I highly suggest using this time matrix and writing down your daily tasks in the appropriate boxes. This way you can prioritize, clarify your values, and compare the worth of your daily activities based on their relationship to those values.

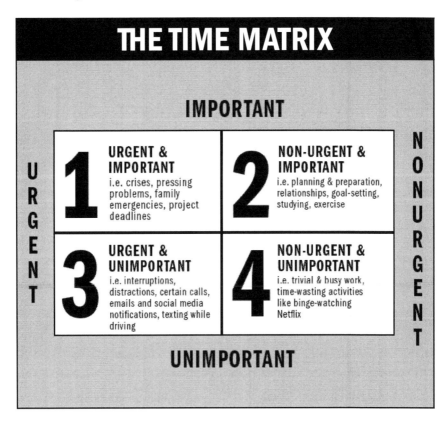

Steven Covey calls it "Putting first things first." That means working on that important paper or handling your business while it's in box 2 and you have time, instead of procrastinating and letting it fall into box 1 the night before it's due. Eighty percent of results flow out of 20 percent of the activities. So much depends on you recognizing your priorities and being able to say "no" or "later" to things that are unimportant. And the way you say "no" to those things is by having a bigger YES burning inside. If we don't have a clear idea of what's important —the results we desire in our lives — we are easily diverted into responding to the urgent. The way you spend your time is a result of the way you see your priorities, so I hope you will use the time matrix and get clear on the things that matter most in your life and take care of them first.

MENTAL EXERCISE

As a life-long student, it's important to remain active. You should treat your brain like a muscle and exercise it daily. Evidence suggests that when your brain is stimulated through exercises that challenge you mentally, it improves your brain function and reduces the risk of declines in cognitive or mental processes like perception, judgment, reasoning and memory. Mental stimulation helps the brain grow stronger, faster and better equipped to handle all of life's positions and daily tasks you might be charged with.

Mental exercises are anything that stimulates you to think; it could be starting a good conversation with a friend or interesting person. Some conversations are more stimulating than others; debating who should win on the "Bachelor" is much less stimulating than discussing the pros and cons of The Affordable Care Act or brainstorming new solutions to a life-challenge. Reading a good book is another great way to stimulate your mind and grow in life. Some of the greatest lessons I've learned in life were from a great book. Reading not only stimulates the brain by forcing it to analyze words, sentence structure and storyline, but it also stimulates our imagination. It causes our brain to make mental images as we read in order to interpret the story. Your brain is constantly at work as you're reading, and reading is a great way to continue life as a student.

Playing games is another way to stimulate your mind. Although video games like Angry Birds and Call of Duty are extremely fun and popular, I'm referring to more traditional games that challenge you to problem solve: Scrabble, crossword puzzles, chess, etc. That type of thinking process is a great way to get those brain cells flowing and engaged.

As athletes, what happens when we stop exercising? We start to lose our muscle, our strength and our endurance. Well, never stop learning! You have to be committed to life-long learning.

A great way to navigate through life with the mindset of a student and continue to gain knowledge is to seek the counsel of other people. Borrow other people's knowledge. I call it copying genius! Similar to having a tutor in school, or a coach on the playing field, you can have a mentor in life. Seek people that know the things that you don't and are willing to help you learn. Ask for help, ask for advice, ask for the experiences of others and take notes so you can learn from them! We will go much more in depth into how to gain mentors in the last section of the book—Building Your Roster.

UTILITY WORKOUTS

TEN PAGES A DAY

For the next 30 days, read 10 pages of a good book a day—a book that will stimulate your mind. Here are the top 5 books that changed my life (and I've already mentioned them throughout this book):

- *Think and Grow Rich* by Napoleon Hill
- *The 5 Love Languages* by Gary Chapman
- *The 7 Habits of Highly Effective People* by Stephen Covey
- *How to Win Friends and Influence People* by Dale Carnegie
- *Who Moved My Cheese* by Spencer Johnson

GROW YOUR SKILLS

Write down your top 3 current goals. Take a look at your goals and identify the specific things that will require you to improve your skills in order to reach that goal. Maybe it's a YouTube "How To…" video. Maybe it's more time spent practicing and mastering your skill. Maybe it's reaching out to a mentor and asking for help. Maybe it's reading a book specifically on that skillset you want to improve. Pay particular attention to the things that you're not used to doing, the things that make you uncomfortable. These are usually the things you'll need to begin to practice regularly in order to get better at that skill and reach your goal. Set aside time each day to practice those exercises until you have mastered them. Don't peak! Continue to grow.

COPY GENIUS

Make a list of 5 people you can think of in your life that have a certain skillset or characteristic that you'd like to acquire. Reach out to them and ask them to meet with you so you can learn more about how they do what they do. In Part 4, we will explore more about how to specifically interview mentors for information. Today, just start jotting down the people you want to potentially mentor you.

CHAPTER 10

Be an Athlete

As a utility player in life, you never stop being an athlete. Growing up, I always thought being an athlete meant being on a team, wearing a uniform, or competing in a sport. Now that I am no longer playing sports competitively (with the exception of my super fun co-ed slow pitch softball games on Monday nights), I realize how important it is to stay active, stay motivated and always take care of my body. Although I don't get to suit up anymore for game day, I still exercise daily like I'm training the day before game day! Not to win a trophy, but to conquer my mind, body and soul. Being an athlete goes beyond wearing a jersey and representing a team or school. Playing the position of athlete means your mindset is competitive, motivated and humble. You know the importance of staying active and treating your body with good care, because you only get one! How you treat your body has a direct impact on the quality of life you enjoy, and it's hard to do the things you want in life if your health isn't good. Our bodies require sleep, exercise, clean air, water, and quality nourishment. Luckily for me, I have always been active and enjoyed getting my sweat on, regardless if there was a game on the line or an end goal attached to it. When I was in school, workouts and practice and lifting weights were required, but I enjoyed it. I enjoyed the run tests that we would have after winter break, because I would go home and continue to work out in the off-season, and come back to campus always ready to go. I never lost that exercise mindset even after I retired from sports. It is still a healthy habit that has remained with me, but I know this isn't the case for everyone.

Some people hate to exercise, and dread getting up and moving to the extent of exhausting their body in any way. My advice would be to find an exercise that you like and enjoy; something that is more fun for you. Maybe instead of running, you can pick up dancing or take dance class. Maybe instead of lifting weights at the gym, you can try kickboxing, or cycling. Exercise for me is therapeutic. I usually work out in the mornings; it's the first thing I do to start my day since I don't necessarily have to use my mental space while I work out. I can turn my mind off from thinking about the tasks for the day, and just focus on doing the exercises while I listen to music. It gets my energy up for the day, and I feel rejuvenated and accomplished when I'm finished, which totally gets me prepared to own my day. Switching up my workouts is what helps me stay consistent. I do classes like interval training, kickboxing, cycling, and Orangetheory Fitness. I'm not a big fan of running, so instead I like to jump rope for cardio. I actually use the treadmill for walking, not running... I put it at a high incline and power walk for cardio because that's how much I don't enjoy running. Exercise activities outdoors are also fun for me; I love to go on hikes and bike rides, or play beach volleyball on a nice sunny day. Find what it is that you enjoy that helps you get your body moving and stay physically healthy.

Another way to help yourself stay consistent and disciplined in your exercise is to have a personal trainer, or group fitness, or an exercise buddy—basically, people that can hold you accountable. I've found it much easier to work out when I know someone else is going to be there, or expecting me to be there to work out with them. Having someone or a group of people that can push you and hold you accountable is key to staying encouraged and on track for success.

I used to think that I could eat whatever I wanted as long as I worked out; and for a while, I was doing just that. I would feed my body all types of junk food in high school and my first couple years of college, but work out hard daily and think I would always be able to maintain a healthy and fit body this way. Well unfortunately, that was not the case. I remember one of my teammates and best friends went on this super healthy nutritional lifestyle switch where she no longer ate fast food, or anything with high sugar and processed fats. Watching her pay such close attention to the things she was feeding her body had a huge effect on me. I remember her looking at me and saying, "Marti, you can't just eat whatever you want and work it off and expect to look, feel and be healthy. Fitness is 10% exercise, 10% genetics, and 80% nutrition. Abs are made in the kitchen." This stuck with me and I started to take notice of how I was fueling my body. I started to eliminate things from my diet like soda, and only drank water. I started to cook my meals more rather than eating out (which actually saved me a lot more money as a college student). It's still an ongoing process for me, but the awareness and consciousness I have now when it comes to what food I eat regularly and when I eat it has made a change for the better.

Not only should we approach life as an athlete in a physical sense, but mentally as well. An athlete's mentality is competitive, as they always strive to be their best. John Wooden describes this as "competitive greatness." Competitive greatness isn't about winning or losing; Wooden describes competitive greatness as "the ability to be at your best when your best is needed." Competitive greatness is about approaching challenges and difficult situations as opportunities for growth that don't often occur. Wooden said it best, "There's more pleasure in being involved in something that's difficult than there is in being involved in something that anybody else could do." A lot of the daily tasks that you and I do, anybody else can do most of them. They're easy and mundane, and often there is no joy in those. But there is joy in being involved in something that is more difficult. In all honesty, writing this book has been one of the most difficult challenges of my life. It was something I've never done before, something I truly cared about, and something I wanted to give to others. Because it meant so much to me, I wanted it to be very good so I would constantly find myself over-thinking everything! I would write a page, and erase it, write again and edit it and switch things from one section to another, and try to sit down daily to get in the writing mood. Sometimes the mood just wasn't there and I would stare at the paper for a while just thinking about what I wanted to write, and an hour would go by and I only had written one sentence. Talk about a challenge! But like Wooden said, the athlete in me is a competitor, not against others, but against myself and my own mind. Utility players accept the challenge and the opportunity to become the best version of themselves.

As athletes, we are used to doing the things we need to do or the things we should do, even when we don't feel like it, and that shouldn't change in life off the playing field. An athlete knows how important it is to stay disciplined and motivated. Motivation can easily die if not fed often. I feed my motivation through music, good books, good people, and exercise. I have a playlist of songs that will instantly light a fire inside of me and get me pumped up and ready to tackle any tasks thrown my way. It's similar to what we used during games as we walked up to the plate for an at-bat. We each got to choose our own "walk-out" song. Same with boxers when they come out and walk towards the ring. They have a "walk-out" song. It's something that you get to choose that will instantly get your blood flowing, your heart beat going, and chills running through your body. It's a song that will bring you the confidence you need to fight and not give up.

My "walk out" song was something I took very seriously, and I wanted to make sure it was timeless (like I wouldn't get sick of hearing it, or it wouldn't be played-out on the radio), and it would make everyone stop and listen. My walk-out song was the first 30-35 seconds of "Ready or Not" by the Fugees, and even until this day, that song still puts me in a great mood and gives me chills.

A lot of us function according to how we feel. People act kind and positive when they feel like it. People go to church when they feel like it. People are loving towards their spouse or significant other when they feel like it. People work at being better at a skillset when they feel like it. Reality check, most of the time, you're not going to feel like it. We are emotional human beings. We have to learn how to acknowledge our emotions without being controlled by them. We have to learn to encourage ourselves, and stay motivated, even when we don't feel like it.

When playing the position of athlete, we also must remain humble. One of the biggest life lessons being an athlete taught me was how to bounce back from mistakes, and how to manage failure. Learning from failure can go hand in hand with humility. The topic of failure is such a tough one for me because I'm extremely competitive, driven by the desire to win, and I set extremely high goals to the point that even when I come up short, to everyone else, it's still considered a win.

Because I competed in sports all of my life, and at home I was the youngest of three ultra-competitive siblings, I developed a culture of not just competing, but winning. I used to believe that winning was in my blood. I was so obsessed with winning that there didn't even need to be a prize. I would lay it all on the line just for the sake of winning. This is one of my biggest strengths, but at the same time, my ultimate weakness.

Going from working at Marcus & Millichap, one of the largest real estate investment brokerages in the country, to working at Positive Coaching Alliance, a non-profit organization that elevates the life lessons we learn through sports, has completely changed the course of my thinking when it comes to success versus failure, or winning versus losing. On one hand, I was obsessed with winning and competing, beating you or anyone else that tried to compete against me. And on the other hand, I still compete fiercely, but I focus on the process, the learning experience and growing myself more and more each day. Which hand sounds healthier to you?

> **SIGNIFICANT SUCCESSES ARE PRECEDED BY A SERIES OF CHALLENGES.**

Believe it or not, failure is healthy to overall development. We learn much more from failing than we do from succeeding. If you have two ears and a mouth, you're going to fail at some point. It's inevitable. You're not always going to come out on top 100% of the time, and that's okay! Don't get me wrong, I am not sitting over here asking for failure. I don't pray, "Yes God! Give me failure so I can learn!" No. I am constantly asking for favor in all areas of my life. Let's be real, if I had the choice to win or lose, I pick win every time. But as I think about the significant successes I have accomplished to date, I realize that anything worthwhile that I have ever accomplished took more than one attempt to get it. It never happened overnight. My plans don't always work like I thought they would, but I ask God to teach me and give me the wisdom to recognize and understand how He's working in my life.

FAILURE IS DELAY, NOT DEFEAT!

God had a purpose for your life long before you ever had a plan for yourself. So if your plan has failed, don't trip! Sometimes your plans have to fail so God's purpose can prevail.

Sports taught me at a young age how to manage failure and bounce back; after all, sport is the safest place for kids to fail. I'd rather strike out in a softball game than to not get into the school of my dreams or take an "L" in life.

Our most significant successes are preceded by a series of challenges and attempts that didn't quite produce the results we were initially striving to achieve. I LOVE to win, but the older I get, the more respect I have for failure. I have developed a healthier (it's not quite where it needs to be yet, but it's healthier) respect for failure, seeing it as a part of the continuum to success, not the final result. Remember, the opposite of success is not failure; it's not trying in the first place or it's giving up! Never let a temporary setback be a permanent defeat. Failing is God's way of telling you "keep going, I've got something better for you, but you have to keep going. It'll work out when I tell it to." Motivational speaker, author and consultant Denis Waitley said it best, "Failure should be our teacher, not our undertaker. Failure is delay, not defeat. It is a temporary detour, not a dead end. Failure is something we can avoid only by saying nothing, doing nothing, and being nothing." So if you're not experiencing any type of failure in life, then you're probably just sitting in your comfort zone, not trying to get to another level.

UTILITY WORKOUTS

GUT CHECK

What is the biggest physical challenge that you face? Is it your weight? Is it your personal views on your body image? Is it injury? Disease? Whatever your challenge may be, what would it look like for you to take better care of your body? Write down one step that you can take today towards improving your physical and mental health.

JUNK IN, JUNK OUT

When I was growing up, my dad always used to tell me "junk in, junk out" which means whatever you feed your mind will manifest into your reality. So, if you're feeding your mind junk, it will produce junk. Think about the "junk" in your life. What are the things that you watch, follow on social media, or people that you hang with that have a negative effect on your body image? Go on a binge for the next 30 days from those things and note how you feel.

GET AFTER IT!

Over the next 30 days, spend 30 minutes to 1 hour a day, at least 4 days a week doing some type of physical exercise. Find an accountability partner, or a buddy who is willing to work out with you. Check in with him or her to see your progress.

WALK-OUT SONG

If you had to choose one, what would be your walk-out song? Make a list of the songs that pump you up and get you motivated to face any challenge.

Some of the other songs on my pump up playlist are:

- "3 Peat" by Lil' Wayne
- "Champion" by Kanye West
- "Til I Collapse" by Eminem
- "Numb/Encore" by Jay Z & Linkin Park
- "Thunder" by Imagine Dragons

CHAPTER 11

Be a Professional

A utility player in life also plays the position of professional. I don't necessarily mean professional athlete, although this could be a utility player's profession. When I say "professional" I mean what you do as your career and how you make a living. There comes a time in your life when we have to make a transition into the real world and make decisions on what you would like to do for a living. When you've played sports your entire life, this transition can be very difficult. You might have never had any traditional job experience or worked in a traditional job setting before. You may be dreading this transition and asking yourself, how am I going to make money? What goods or services am I going to provide? What do I even want to do? What am I passionate about? How am I going to compete with the current job market when I feel so behind?

Most people drift through life in a box following a desperate, but common path. Four years of high school, graduate college and then spend the next 10 years jumping from job to job doing things that have nothing to do with the degree they got years before. Then they often revert back to school because they can't decide what they really want to do with their life until they're forced to make a change because the job situation they're in becomes more miserable than the risk of change.

In conversations I have with athletes on their way to future careers after sports, I often hear them say things like, "Outside of my sport, I don't know what I'm good at. I don't know what I'm passionate about other than my sport. This is my identity." This is a tough place to find yourself in when your playing days are over and you have to start making a living. It's always dangerous to wrap your entire identity in something that isn't forever. In something that will eventually come to an end.

BEING AN ATHLETE IS ONLY ONE PART OF YOUR IDENTITY!

Well, being an athlete is only one part of your identity. As we discussed, we play multiple positions in life. And there are things that we learn in each position that can strengthen us for the next position. An athlete might believe that they're no good at anything other than their sport, but there are tons of things within their sport that translate over into so many other areas. Maybe you're a great leader and can handle a management position. Maybe you're a great problem-solver, and can handle a job that requires constant adjustment to changes. Maybe you're a great communicator and relationship builder, which goes well for careers in human relations.

If you played sports and have an athlete's mindset, there are tons of things you can do after your playing days are over. It's not necessarily a matter of if you can do it, it's more of a matter of what you should do outside of your sport. The "what" is the part that people struggle with—not just athletes in transition, but most people in transition. A lot of people work for a living, but only few people work for their passions and truly love what they do. I know what you're thinking: "Marti, how does one go about finding their passion?" Great question! I'm glad you asked! I wish there was an easy way to find out exactly what you want to do with your life, but unfortunately, it is something that may take a while. But don't trip; there are definitely ways to get started on launching a passion-based life. Here's what I suggest—spend some time on this exercise (trust me; you'll be happy you did!)

KNOW YOURSELF

What are your values/beliefs? What do you care about? What are your hobbies and interests? What subject do you never shut up about? How do you love to spend your time? Journal your answers to these questions.

KNOW YOUR STRENGTHS

What are you good at? What do other people (friends, family, professors, teachers, coaches, baby daddies…) say you're good at? Make a list of your strengths.

TAKE WORRIES AND FEAR OUT OF THE EQUATION

If you could do anything but fail, what would you do and why? (Just brainstorm with no voice of criticism to hold you back.)

If money wasn't an option, meaning, if you had to work for free/ain't getting paid a dime what would you be doing? Or in other words—if all jobs paid the same, what would you be doing? In the words of Kid

President, "What will you create to make the world more awesome?"

Now, go back and answer the previous questions truthfully. Our passions are often irrational and at war with logic and reason, so we push our first option aside quickly because it seems unrealistic or we think we can't make good money doing it? NONSENSE! Truly think with your heart when you're answering the previous three questions. That's right. Do this exercise again.

LOVE WHAT YOU DO

If you don't like doing something, you can do one of two things: You can stop doing it (quit, delegate it, hire it out) OR you can figure out how to love it with all of your heart. Bring passion into the things you're already doing. Commit to loving everything you do. You may not always be able to change what you're doing, but you can always change how you do it or the state of mind you're doing it in. Life's too short to whine and complain about how miserable your circumstance is—change your circumstance or change your mind! Start taking responsibility for your experiences.

Back in December of 2013, I followed a process just like the one above and, without exaggeration, it changed the course of my life. The insight I gained led me to leave my brokerage business and pursue my passions — inspiring young dreamers, traveling and working with athletes. Because I stopped working for a living and started working for my passions, I was presented with the opportunity to join Positive Coaching Alliance as their Partnership Manager for the Southern California region; a "from-home" job that allowed me to travel, and is tailor-made to my passions, desires, and the impact I was called to leave on the world! Since 2014, I've grown and been promoted with Positive

Coaching Alliance and have found happiness in my career. It's crazy how the divine power of the universe, the good Lord almighty starts to manifest when you lead with your passions. I hope this inspires you to find your passions and start living them with all of your heart.

CAREER CAPITAL

I am extremely grateful to work for an organization that is tailor-made to my passions, skills, and the impact I was called to make in the lives of others. There's a really cool concept I learned from my mastermind group called "career capital." It's not easy to find career capital, but once you've found it, hold on tight!

Career capital is basically made up of three things, and the more of these three things you have in your career, the higher your career capital.

1) PURPOSE/MEANING: a sense that what you're doing is making some kind of impact in some kind of way. Does what you do make a difference in this world or on the people in it? Do you feel like what you do is important?

2) AUTONOMY: a sense of freedom and control over what you're doing; the freedom to make your own decisions. Do you have the ability to do, go or create as you wish with those you choose to work with?

3) SPECIALIZATION: the progressive realization of mastery or growth in a certain skill that you bring to the table. Are you using a skillset that you offer better than anyone else? Are you the expert in your field, and if not, does your work allow you to grow in the skills you need to become an expert? When your work allows you to do something you're really good at, your career capital will go higher.

The unique thing about career capital is that it has nothing to do with the amount of money you make. Although the amount of money an occupation offers is very attractive, don't let it cloud your judgement on what you decide to do with your life. I've learned that the amount of career capital you grow is more important than the amount of financial capital, because career capital has a direct correlation to the amount of love you have for what you do, while financial capital has an indirect connection. When making a decision about new job opportunities, make sure to measure the career capital you will receive.

To succeed as a utility player, you must remain committed, hardworking and positive. I was watching an interview with Will Smith, one of my favorite actors, and I couldn't believe how committed he was to achieving the things he set out to achieve. He said, "The only thing that I see that is distinctly different about me is I'm not afraid to die on a treadmill. I will not be out-worked, period. You might have more talent than me, you might be smarter than me, you might be sexier than me, you might be all of those things you got it on me in nine categories. But if we get on the treadmill together, there's two things: You're getting off first, or I'm going to die. It's really that simple." Isn't it safe to say that if he's willing to DIE, he's pretty committed?

COMMITMENT INVOLVES SACRIFICE.

How committed are you to your goals? dreams? health? relationships? Are you willing to die on a treadmill for what you want? Commitment is probably the NUMBER ONE thing that separates you from achieving what you're hungry for. Yes, there are things in life that we want to happen, but simply wanting it to happen means that you'll do it when circumstances permit.

Commitment means an unwavering YES. It means we're willing to give 100% of everything we've got and do whatever it takes to make something happen, no matter the circumstances, the odds, the personal gain or recognition, no matter the comfort or level of difficulty—you are going to do it REGARDLESS. Again, I ask, how committed are you?

One of the first keys to true commitment is a burning desire. You have to have meaning and purpose in order to want something so bad that it burns inside of you. Your burning desire is what gets you out of bed every day on a mission to achieve what you said you were going to achieve yesterday. Be clear on your goals and what you want to achieve. It's hard to stay committed to something you're not absolutely clear about. Would you run a marathon without a finish line? I know I wouldn't. In order to stay the course, in order to remain absolutely committed to something, you must be clear on what it is you want to achieve and don't stop until you get there.

Commitment involves sacrifice. True commitment means you're willing to give up the things that are valued but don't matter as much as the things you're committed to. The things you are committed to will cause interruptions in some areas of your life, but you can tell how committed someone is by how easy it is to distract them or convince them otherwise.

At the center of bringing dreams to fruition is self-discipline, but the majority of people are not willing to do what it takes to get where they want to go or be what they want to be. The Marines have a saying

"Everyone wants to go to heaven, but nobody wants to die." When you develop self-discipline, you gain control of your mind to always choose the actions that are in your best interest to achieving your goals.

Commitment is not easy. Let's face it, our enthusiasm to achieve something will not be at the same level every single day, and if you are human, there's this thing I call the New Year's Resolution Effect that you and I can fall into. You know how New Year's comes and we make these resolutions and we're ON FIRE and excited and determined for the next 2-3 maybe even 4 weeks to act? But a month later the passion has died and we have dropped the ball. That will happen to you if you do not set up an accountability system for yourself. You have to hold yourself accountable daily to the things you're trying to achieve in the future. You also hold yourself accountable by telling your closest friends and family about the things you're trying to achieve. Whether their reactions are positive or negative doesn't matter, letting others know will help you stay accountable. Also, join a group of people that can hold you to your word. Surround yourself with like-minded individuals who are rooting for you to succeed and it will drive you even further to stay committed.

The first job I landed out of college was, at the time, my dream job. I was working for the top real estate investment company in the country without any real estate experience, but let me tell you how I went about getting that job. Like I mentioned before, I was pretty money hungry when I graduated from college; I was ready to start making BANK so I wanted to get into commercial real estate and start making six figures within two years out of school.

I knew I didn't have any real estate experience so I did my research to find out what's the top real estate firm in the country with the best training for new hires. I found out that was Marcus & Millichap (M&M). People that come out of their training end up starting their own real estate brokerages and a ton of M&M's competitors, like CB Richard Ellis, started at Marcus & Millichap. I saw an opportunity through our internal job network at UCLA for an internship in the downtown Long Beach office of M&M and I thought, "Perfect!" That's my hometown, it's 10 minutes away from my house; this couldn't be more perfect. I sent in my resume and I got one of those automated responses saying "Thank you for your interest; please give me a call to discuss your future with Marcus & Millichap. Signed, Mr. Manager" (I'll keep his name confidential). I called him. They said he was in a meeting but they would forward me to his voicemail. I left a voicemail, "Hello Mr. Manager, my name is Marti Reed, I just sent you my resume and I was calling because I am very interested in interning for Marcus & Millichap in the downtown Long Beach office after I graduate from UCLA in the spring. Please give me a call back when you have a moment. Thanks!"

The next day I called again and again, he was unavailable. They directed me to voicemail but I didn't leave a message because I had left one the day before and he might not have heard it yet; so I hung up. The next day, still no sign of Mr. Manager, so I call again. They directed me to voicemail again so I left another message. I'm thinking to myself, he's probably had a chance to listen to his messages by now so I want him to know I'm serious. I left another message, "Hey Mr. Manager, Marti Reed again from UCLA trying to reach you about the intern position at M&M, please give me a call when you have a chance. If you catch my voicemail, it's probably because I'm at softball practice and just missed your call, but please get back to me when you can. Thanks!"

You see what I did? I kept mentioning things that would hopefully grab his interest and make him want to call me back. UCLA…softball practice…after I graduate in the spring. It wasn't working though, because about a month and seven voicemails later, I still hadn't heard from him. It was time for Plan B. How am I going to get my foot in this door? I wondered. I've heard that we are only seven circles away from meeting anyone we want to meet in the world; which means connections and networking can lead you anywhere. Well, I didn't know anyone at M&M, I already checked. But at the time, I had over 20 mentors, so I figured I had to know somebody that knew somebody that knew something about M&M.

So, I called one of my mentors who was a big-time restaurant owner. He owned King's Seafood in downtown Long Beach, which is right up the street from the World Trade Center building where M&M is located. I asked him if he knew anyone at M&M. He said no, but he would check with his friend. "Remember the young lady I introduced you to a couple of years ago who wanted to go to UCLA so I had her talk to you for some advice?" he asked.

I was thinking in my head, "Yes! Thank God I took the time to chat with her and help her out."

"Well, her dad is the president of Downtown Long Beach Business Association and probably knows people at M&M," he added.

I reached out to the President of Downtown LB Business Association per my mentor's connection and asked him if he knew anyone at M&M. "Yes! My good friend works for M&M," he said. "I'll set you up with a meeting!"

So I got my foot in the door for an informational interview with a senior broker (this is still not the manager; it's not the person that hires and fires people) but I sat down with him to ask him questions about M&M and what it takes to be a broker. We hit it off pretty well because I asked good questions and let him do most of the talking. He put in a word for me to the manager; his boss who never returned my calls. Finally, about two days later my phone rang and it was Mr. Manager. He was not easy to talk to over the phone. He hammered me with questions like "Why would I hire you? You don't have any real estate experience. Why do you even want to be a broker? It sounds like to me you just want a job." It was one of the most difficult and uncomfortable phone calls I've ever had with a potential employer. The most encouraging thing he said was that my resume was "not that bad." It was clear that he had no interest in meeting or hiring me, but nonetheless, he agreed to bring me in for an interview after my softball season finished.

When the time came to set up the interview, once again, Mr. Manager would not call me back. After a couple weeks of more voicemails, I finally hit up the broker I met with before. I let him know that Mr. Manager wasn't answering my phone calls even after he said he would bring me in for an interview. The broker agreed to speak with Mr. Manager and get back to me. The broker emailed me the next day explaining that Mr. Manager was looking to hire someone with a couple years of experience in the brokerage business and didn't want to train someone completely new.

It sounds ridiculous, but I actually felt awful for not having years of experience for an intern position. I persisted. In an email to Mr. Manager I wrote: "I hear that you are looking for someone with more experience in the brokerage business, and if that's the case, I understand that I am not the right fit right now. I would still like to sit down with you because I value your opinion and I'd like to know what it would take for me to be able to gain the experience and best prepare myself to come back and work for M&M in the future." With this approach, I got the meeting. He gave me a date and time to come in for an informational interview to ask him questions for 15 minutes (he was very clear on the time frame). I went in to do my informational interview, taking the same approach of being interested more than interesting—asking good questions and letting Mr. Manager do the majority of the talking. The meeting lasted an hour and a half, and by the time I walked out of there, he offered me 2 positions—junior broker or personal assistant. He told me he had been considering stepping down from the manager position to be a senior broker, and at that time he would want to have me on his team as either his executive assistant or junior broker. The rest is history.

When it comes to nailing the job, you have to get creative— think outside of the box. If you want something you've never had, you've got to do something you've never done. I had no real estate experience, but I was persistent and committed. I had confidence in my ability to be coachable, learn, and outwork those with experience. Sports is where I learned these traits. I would not know how to be competitive in life if it wasn't for the experiences I had competing as an athlete. Don't be afraid to take chances, even when the odds are completely against you. Where there's a will, there's a way—and sometimes, you just have to make a way.

THE OBSTACLE IS THE PATH

I, along with a lot of other people, used to feel that challenges and obstacles standing in the way of my goals were "blocking my way on the path." I always looked at obstacles as these huge dreadful hindrances interrupting my plans, and I thought that I would have to find a way around them in order to get to where I wanted to go. One of my mentors told me that's not true. He said, "Marti, obstacles don't block you on the path, they are the path." At first I didn't understand what he meant. How can an obstacle be the path to reach my goals, when all they do is slow me down? Then he broke it down for me so I could understand.

If your goal is to get to the moon, but the obstacle is that you don't have a rocket ship, then your path becomes getting or building a rocket ship. Some people let the obstacles stop them from achieving their goal: "I would go to the moon, but I don't have a rocket ship." But others take obstacles as clues on how to actually get to the goal: "I see that I will need a rocket ship. How can I get one?" When I was a student-athlete, my goal and a lot of my teammate's goal was to get good grades or a certain GPA in school. If you got a 3.0 last semester, your success on getting a 4.0 this semester would be correctly identifying which obstacles stopped you last semester. Did you go to all of your classes last semester? If not, that's one obstacle you can eliminate this semester—go to class! Start identifying all the obstacles that stopped you last semester and you will have a clear path on what to do this semester; you can start knocking those obstacles down one by one.

When I first arrived at UCLA, I was more of a "line-drive" hitter as opposed to a home-run hitter. In high school, I had a high batting average, but it was mostly from hitting singles and doubles, with a home run every once in a while. I was tall and thin. I didn't hit the ball the furthest, but I would hit it hard and use my speed to run fast around the bases. When I got to UCLA, my goal was to crack the starting line-up, but I found myself on the bench behind a group of girls that could all hit the ball so far—they were home run hitters. They would hit the ball consistently over the fence. I started to realize that my style of hitting was holding me back from achieving my goal of making the starting line-up. I began to use the obstacle as the path. I started bulking up in the weight room to get stronger and more powerful. I changed my swing to be more linear than rotational in order to put more of my strength and weight into the ball. I started hitting the ball much farther, further than I'd ever hit the ball before. Once I started hitting the ball out of the park consistently in practice, I got noticed more by the coaches, more playing time opportunities, and eventually made the starting line-up.

Why let obstacles stand in your way to reach your goals when they can be the way? When you know what's stopping you, you can have a clear path for what to do next. In this way, the obstacle is the path. It's inevitable that obstacles are going to occur in your life, so use them to your advantage and start achieving your biggest goals and dreams.

UTILITY WORKOUTS

SUPER-CHARGE YOUR GOALS

The first step is to put your goals on paper. Write them down in first person, present tense, positive language. Say what you WILL DO, not what you won't. Your goals should sound as if they have already happened. For example, if my goal is to have an A in Chemistry class by the end of the school year, my goal will sound something like this: "On May 30th, I am an A student in my Chemistry class."

Review your goals daily. Literally, carry them with you! Post them in places where you can see them on a daily basis. Mine are above my mirror, in my shower, in my wallet, in my car—I can't hide from them. Read them out loud multiple times a day — when you wake up and before you go to sleep. I'm serious. It becomes a self-fulfilling prophecy when you are affirming your goals and speaking them into existence.

THE OBSTACLE IS THE PATH

Here is a step by step way to use obstacles as the path to your goals.

1. Write down your most important goal.
2. List all of the obstacles in your way.
3. Circle the top 2 critical obstacles.
4. What tools do you have available to overcome these obstacles? (i.e. books, mentors, friends, technology, your habits, process, informational interviews, developing a new skill, time commitment, etc.)
5. What next action will you take today?
6. Repeat until there are no more obstacles left standing in your way.

BUILD A PERSONAL PORTFOLIO

A personal portfolio is simply a book of your achievements, highlights and experiences that will help someone want to get to know you better. It's the concept of pre-heating. There's a natural law out there that people believe more of what they hear about you, than what they hear directly from you. Creating a personal portfolio to give to a potential employer of a company you are interested in, or to the board of a non-profit you'd like to be involved with, or to the landlord of a building you'd like to rent—whoever you're trying to impress, the portfolio will separate you from the rest of the pack and put you in a position to be remembered. It's like a resume on steroids.

You will need: A 1.5" 3 ring binder, plastic sheet protectors, a scanner, a computer with Microsoft Word or PowerPoint, a printer, a blue ink pen, and your awards/pictures/letters of recommendation/ newspaper clippings/anything else you want to show off.

Please refer to the back of the book in Appendix C to see the full instructions on how to create your personal portfolio.

CREATE A VISION MAP

Vision mapping is something I learned in Steven K. Scott's book, The Richest Man Who Ever Lived. Vision mapping is the process of writing a clear and specific vision with a detailed road map to achieving your vision.

Step 1: Write a clear and precise description of the vision. Make it as descriptive as possible; you can even describe the day outside and the clothes you're wearing in the vision. Turn on your childlike imagination and make it as vivid as possible.

Step 2: List your goals. One goal per page. Refer to the first Utility Workout in this chapter of super-charging your goals to make sure your goals are written the right way.

Step 3: Turn your goals into steps. Under each goal, break down the steps that will be needed in order to reach those goals.

Step 4: Turn your steps into tasks. Under each step, list the daily tasks that are needed to complete the steps.

Step 5: Set deadlines. Go back to each step and task and set a deadline of completion in order to hold yourself accountable. This will help you do everything one step at a time, piece by piece until all of your goals are achieved.

Step 6: Create a vision board. Bring your vision to life with a collage. Use magazines, photographs, catalogues, anything that inspires you and reminds you of your goals. Cut out images and words and glue them on a large piece of poster board. Hang this board up in a place where you can see it every day and visualize your goals and dreams with the images. Mine is hanging right above the light switch when I enter my bedroom. When I was in college, I laminated it and hung it in my shower where I could stare at it every day.

CHAPTER 12

Be a Community Member

There once was a businessman visiting a resort community for a conference, and he left his hotel early one morning to take a walk along the beach. When he arrived at the shoreline, he noticed a shocking sight. Countless starfish were lying on the beach that had been washed up in a high tide during the night. They were still alive and moving, climbing all over each other trying to get back into the ocean. The man looked up and knew it wouldn't be long before the sun fully came out and the poor creatures would bake to death as they were trapped there on the sand. There were thousands of starfish as far as his eye could see, and he wished he could do something about it, but there was no way he could make a dent in saving them. So, he continued on his way in dismay. As he walked further along the beach, he came across a young boy who he saw lean over, scoop up a starfish, and fling it like a Frisbee into the ocean. He watched as the little boy continued this process over and over again, picking up speed with each starfish he flung, clearly trying to save their lives. Once the man realized what the boy was doing, he felt sorry for the kid, and felt like it was his responsibility to share a harsh life lesson with the boy. He approached the little boy and said, "Son, I see what you are doing here and let me tell you, it's very noble, but you can't save all of these starfish. There are thousands of them. The sun's getting really hot and there's not enough time; unfortunately, they're all going to die. You'll be better off just going on your way to go play or something, you really can't make much of a difference here." The little boy stopped and didn't say anything at first; he just stared back at the businessman as he thought of the news that was just shared with him. Then the boy leaned down again and picked up another starfish, flung it out into the ocean as far as he could and said, "Well I just made all the difference for that one." I think Helen Keller sums this lesson up best when she says; "I am only one, but still I am one. I cannot do everything, but I still can do something; and because I cannot do everything, I will not refuse to do something that I can do."

The little boy didn't allow the magnitude of his situation to stop him from doing all that he could do to make a difference: save one starfish at a time. Sometimes we can look at the magnitude of the ugliness going on in the world (mass murders, world hunger, AIDS epidemic, war on drugs, human trafficking, global warming, political change, etc.) and think, "these issues are so enormous and complex that I'll never make a difference, so why even bother trying?" But if we make it a habit to do what we can, when we can, where we can with what we have, not only can at least one life be transformed, but our life will be transformed as well. We can all make a difference, if we approach it one starfish at a time.

During a Q & A session at a large conference, John C Maxwell, the great author, speaker and expert on leadership was asked, "What has been your greatest challenge as a leader?" To most of the audience's dismay he answered "leading me!" The truth is, we are all leaders, because it is our responsibility to lead ourselves first before we can lead others.

It all begins with you. In order to lead and have influence in a positive, productive, vision-driven direction, you must begin with you. If you want to be a role model and have impact and influence on your community, you must have a willingness to sacrifice personal interests or glory for the welfare of all. You must be prepared to lead by example.

When I played softball at UCLA, we used to watch video of ourselves playing to see what we were doing right, what we were doing wrong, and what we could improve on. I remember one time my coach was telling me that I needed to hold my hands a little lower in my batting stance to be quicker to the ball. When I would go up to bat and I would think that my hands were in the zone, but I still wasn't getting the results. My coach would say, "Marti, you need to get your hands in the zone!" I could've sworn I was doing it! I was thinking, "I am! I have my hands in the zone." Then my coach busted out the video. To my dismay, my hands where nowhere near the zone! You see, what we think we're doing isn't always congruent with reality. Just like athletes watch video to evaluate performance, we have to find ways to look in the mirror and evaluate ourselves accurately.

Let's have a self-evaluation.

Over time I've held many leadership roles. Years of interacting with people has taught me a considerable truth: people seldom see themselves realistically. We do a fine job at evaluating others but we tend to have a hard time evaluating ourselves by the same standards. Most people use a completely different set of criteria for judging themselves than they do when judging others. We judge others according to their actions. But we judge ourselves according to our intentions. So even when we do the wrong thing, we let ourselves off of the hook if we believe our intentions are good. We inflate our own egos to see ourselves more positively, but at the price of putting others down in comparison.

Surprisingly, most of the ugliness we see in others is a reflection of our own nature. I always say the way people talk about others says a lot about themselves — more than it says about the person they are talking about. Do you have friends that you notice are always talking smack, or talking negatively about other people or situations? Those friends that always can find something bad to say. That says a lot about how they feel inside. Those that normally talk well about others and find the good in situations are usually happier inside.

In sports, when you focus on comparison with others, you spend less time mastering your skills and being the best player you can be for your team. One of the beautiful things about competition is the way it can bring out the best in us and totally help us as athletes to raise the bar. Worthy competition can help you rise to another level that you may not have accessed alone. This is a gift that sport gives you, but at the same time, you must not let competition lead to comparison. When athletes start to turn inward and compare or measure up our skills to teammates or opponents, that focus can cause us to spiral in our mental game and affect our performance out on the playing field.

When we compare ourselves to others, usually it stems from one of two things: we perceive the other person to be far ahead of where we are and we feel discouraged, or we perceive our self to be better than the other person and we become proud.

Neither option is good for us. Neither will help us grow on or off of the playing field. Let's not be people that compare ourselves to others, but instead, be utility players that champion each other. This is the better way to play.

ACCEPT YOURSELF (and the gifts you were blessed with)

Say "goodbye" to perfect and "hello" to yourself. Discover who you are and who you want to be. If you don't like something about yourself, work to make it better. At the same time, understand that we are each uniquely gifted. Your gifts are different than mine, and my gifts are different than yours. There is greatness inside all of us and every one of us can decide to wake up every day and strive to be the best version of ourselves.

HAVE COMPASSION

Be kind to yourself and others. Always come from a place of love. When considering someone else's struggles and restoration, remember your own failings and be more understanding towards them. Recognize our common humanity instead of feeling superior or exempt from certain experiences. In the words of Abraham Lincoln, "Don't criticize them; they are just what we would be under similar circumstances."

BE MINDFUL

Have a balanced awareness in life. You never know what someone may be going through. Even if others are unkind, never be the reason for someone to stop shining.

The next time you think about putting someone else down to build yourself up, pump the breaks and think about trying a different way, because your judgment of others speaks volumes on where you are in your own journey. And when you really think about it, the only person you should be evaluating is yourself.

As a community member, we must be faithful, serving and generous. When you are able to give back to your community, you are recognizing that you are a part of something bigger than yourself. Just like in sports, we play for the team. We represent our school and the name on the front of the jersey, rather than focusing on the name on the back.

One of the things that I loved about being a UCLA Bruin was the community and school pride. We respected our school and the community and wanted to represent it with dignity and class. Now that I am a part of a larger community, I want to make sure that I am making the community better than how I entered it. This means focusing on ways I can improve my community, the place I live and the people around me. A utility player sees their community as their team.

UTILITY WORKOUTS

CHOOSE YOUR STARFISH

How often do you let opportunities for impact pass you by because you feel your contribution would be too small? What are the "starfish" situations in your life? List out causes that you feel are too big for you to have a noticeable impact. For the next month, choose one item of comfort, luxury or convenience that you can go without (i.e. Starbucks coffee, your favorite dessert, the extra guac, that show you binge watch on Netflix, etc.) and use that money or time towards one of the causes from your list. Even a small impact makes a big difference.

PART

BUILD YOUR ROSTER

CHAPTER 13

Why Build Your Roster

Imagine you are creating an all-star team filled with the best of the best players. These players must be high-quality, supportive of each other, work hard and make each other better. Each player equally wants to be a part of the team. Who would you put on that roster? How would you go about selecting your players? What qualities do you want the players to have and what culture do you want to create for your team? How would you build your squad? Can you imagine it?

Just like a coach needs to build a team to compete in games, or as a CEO needs to build a workforce to grow a company, we need to build a squad of people in our lives to help us grow and succeed. Building your roster means surrounding yourself with people that you can trust and people that support you, hold you accountable, challenge you, motivate you and help you reach your potential. They tell you what you need to hear and not just what you want to hear.

Building your roster is more than networking. It's more than seeking out mentors. Building your roster means actively and consciously selecting the type of energy you want in your life. Building your roster means attracting the right people as you constantly work on becoming the person you want to attract. From the people you have in your inner circle to the people you choose to follow on social media, anyone taking up space in your mind, thoughts or energy needs to earn their place on your roster.

Have you ever heard of the saying "birds of a feather flock together?" Believe it or not, we are influenced by the things around us—the things we choose to listen to, the books we choose to read, the things we choose to watch, and most importantly, the people we choose to hang with and follow. Your roster has a direct impact on who you are and who you're becoming.

If birds of a feather flock together, you want to flock with eagles and let the turkeys go. Eagles have clear vision. They're fearless, tenacious, filled with vitality, and most importantly, they soar higher than any other bird. Turkeys on the other hand, produce crap, eat their own feces, and are pretty much the dumbest birds ever (Disclaimer: I have nothing against the actual turkey bird; just go with it for the metaphor. Thanks).

It is important to consciously build your roster, because the people and things we surround ourselves with are what we eventually become.

There are eagles and turkeys all around us. There are positive people that dream, produce greatness, soar high and lift others up with them. They add value to our lives and the lives of others. Then there are negative people—the ones that just suck the life out of you, create drama, and tend to bring you down with them.

Our success is highly dependent on our roster. No one has ever achieved anything truly great without the help and the company of others. At the same time, no one has truly failed without the help and company of others. Now, think about the company that you keep and the people in your life. My mom used to always tell me, "Show me your friends and I'll show you your future." Ask yourself, who are the people that are in my life frequently? Who are the people I'm following and are they adding value to the person I want to be? Are they contributing and helping me reach my goals, or are they holding me back? Are they a positive influence in my life or a negative one? Do they deserve a spot on my roster?

Also ask yourself, what type of person am I being to others? Am I being that eagle that they should flock with? Am I lifting them up—encouraging them? Or am I pulling them down?

Unfortunately, not everyone is here for your well-being. Not everyone has your best interest at heart. Not everyone should be on your roster. You should be careful who you choose to flock with. Be careful of those you let into your inner circle. Be careful in who you allow a spot on your roster.

Think about it. Why should you let someone walk with you through your life's journey if they have no intentions of seeing you succeed, seeing you get better, or seeing you reach that next level that you have been trying to reach?

Some of you may be reading this and thinking "Aw man, I've gotta call Felicia up and tell her I said... BYE!" Don't get me wrong, I'm not saying you should just drop all of your friends and cut everyone off that isn't producing in life. I do believe there is value in being the light for someone that is struggling or needs to make better decisions, but only to the extent that it is not going to hold you back from where you're going or derail you from who you're becoming. You can't be any help to anyone else if you're not the best version of yourself that you can be.

Some of us have some turkey friends or even family that we go way back with. They're just chilling taking up all kinds of space on our roster, and it's hard to let them go. We really care about them, and they may start to judge us or say, "Oh you think you're better than us?" You just simply reply, "No, that is not the case. I'm just after something different." Plain and simple. And if they want to grow with you and start making eagle-like contributions, then you can choose to flock with them. But if they make the decision to live a turkey life when they know better, then it's time to walk away from them. Take them off your roster, or put them on the reserve list until they get their act together.

Building your roster is an ongoing process. It doesn't happen overnight. Just like producing anything great, building your roster takes time. It takes energy, it takes practice, but the outcome is well worth the effort.

Here are some key things that will help you start actively building your roster.

KNOW YOURSELF AND NEVER STOP GROWING

Once you are clear on who you want to be, never stop working on it. I'm talking about your core values, interest and goals; I'm talking about the person you are becoming and want to become. If you are clear on this, then it will be easier to attract the people in your life that share those values. Adding them on your roster will be a mutually beneficial decision. The best roster players are ones that share your core values and can understand and relate to your interests and goals. In order for us to build a solid roster and create the levels of personal, professional, or financial success that we desire, we must first commit to dedicating time each and every day to becoming the person we need to be; one who is qualified and capable of consistently attracting, creating and sustaining the roster we want to have. Attract the people you want in your life by becoming attractive.

CONCENTRATE ON WHAT YOU CAN GIVE

Ask yourself, what can I do to help others? How can I bring value? It's important to take analysis of yourself, your talents and capabilities, then you'll figure out what you can offer, and plan ways and means of giving others advantages, services, and ideas that you believe you can successfully deliver.

DON'T BE AFRAID TO SAY "HELLO" TO ANYONE!

Networking is the name of the game. Your opportunities won't increase until your contacts increase. Everyone is unique in their own way and has something to offer this world, so tap into your bold courage. Start simple with "Hi, my name is…" Then get a conversation going by building rapport and asking good questions. Remember, it's better to be interested than interesting. Listen well and praise others more than praising yourself.

SEEK MENTORS

I can't stress this enough, but having a mentor, or a person that has already successfully done something that you would like to do (whether professional or personal) and is willing to share with you how they did it, is so important. The fastest way to learn is not by your own experiences, but by the experiences of other people. A mentor can be a parent, a teacher, a coach, the guy at the bus stop—anyone that can provide needed insight, advice, wisdom or any practical help for effectively achieving your goals and dreams. If you want to get further than where you are right now, you need to seek counsel and guidance from those who are where you want to be.

CHAPTER

Mentors and Networking

I humbly admit that I do not know everything or have all of the answers, but a simple way that I am able to enlarge my scope and gain more clarity in my life, is to tap into the clarity of others that see further than I am able. Here are some tips and strategies to help you identify and effectively gain mentors:

Step 1: Know what you want—determine the specific dream or area in your life in which you'd like a mentor. Remember, the world will step aside for those that know where they are going, so know what you want and why you want it.

Step 2: Create a list of potential mentors for each of these areas or dreams—think about people that you respect most (whether you know them or not). It can be a boss, acquaintance, friend, or even a total stranger. Who might be able to give you advice, wisdom and insight in each area?

Step 3: Research everything you can about the potential mentors on your list. Research their likes, dislikes, passions, experiences—

research anything from personal experiences to second or third-hand knowledge. I'm serious, you need to put on your Olivia Pope gladiator hat and get to work!

Step 4: Prepare to contact the potential mentor with a brief proposal/request. If they're just strangers to you, do you know anyone they know? If so, have that person put in a good word (or pre-heat) for you and make sure to mention that person in your opening line when you reach out. Then express the qualities you admire in the potential mentor, why those qualities are so important to you and how you'd like to gain insight and wisdom in making those special qualities a part of your life. Request a brief amount of time each month where you can ask questions that'll help you grow in those areas.

Here's a sample email that you can customize to send to a potential mentor:

"Dear _____, I received your contact information from my good friend Mrs. Brown, and she suggested that I reach out to you and connect. I am a former UCLA athlete working full-time in a non-profit, helping to develop athletes in character and leadership on and off the field. I am also very interested in real estate development and would like to start purchasing investment property. I admire your experience in real estate development and how you've grown a diverse portfolio with an emphasis on giving back to the community. Your passion and wisdom to create opportunities that advance others in the real estate community is something I wish to learn as I get started. Would you be willing to meet with me for coffee in the next few weeks so I can learn more about how you got started? Thanks so much for your time and consideration."

Step 5: Contact the mentor. Ask for a personal appointment with the mentor. Treat them to breakfast or coffee (it's the cheapest meal and you're paying for it). If you can't make a face-to-face appointment, then the next best thing would be a phone or video call. Keep it brief and to the point because mentors are usually busy (unless they are retired).

Step 6: Follow up. After you've made the first contact, follow up with a short letter of appreciation that recognizes something specific that he/she said or did. If this mentor is the right fit for you, continue to consistently contact them with updates and meetings.

Step 7: REPEAT. Go back to step 2 to get the next person on the list of potential mentors and repeat steps 3-6.

Other important things to remember: Please be careful when choosing a mentor. Just as the right mentor or partner can take you to another level of extraordinary success, the wrong kind of mentor or partner can make your life miserable (this is true in business and marriage…#realtalk). When looking for mentors, do your due diligence first! Avoid red flags (i.e. lack of integrity, disregard for rules/regulations/personal boundaries, gossipers, quick tempers, foolishness, and anyone who offers a lot for a little). You must examine their "walk" before you listen to their talk! Once you've selected your mentors, make sure you are clear and up-front about the goals for the relationship. Always keep it professional. You are in the driver's seat. This means it's not your mentor's job to check in, find you and see if you've made progress. Mentors will offer you information, support, feedback, contacts and ideas, but it's up to YOU to take the initiative. Always show respect for your mentor and his/her time. They will be as effective as you allow them to be.

For all of those graduating and getting ready to embark on the next journey—entering the real world, getting a job, and having a strong and prosperous professional career can be a scary thing to think about. Nonetheless, it is also a chance and an opportunity to grow and become something more than who you are today. In order to get where you want to go in life, you must be able to network. You will not be able to achieve great things without the help of others, and your career opportunities and income will not increase until your contacts increase. What do you do when you are in a room full of people that are each unique in their own way, and each have something to offer this wonderful world we live in? You need to learn how to network in order to increase your contacts and build lasting relationships that will help you achieve your dreams.

THE 4 SIMPLE STEPS TO IN-PERSON NETWORKING

1) INTRODUCE YOURSELF

This is probably the hardest step in these four simple steps of networking. Sometimes having insane courage to approach someone you are interested in getting to know and simply saying, "Hi my name is…" can be the most terrifying thing for some people. But remember, magic happens when you step out of your comfort zone. When you approach someone with a genuine smile, firm handshake and speak up, they will be more impressed with your ability to take initiative and begin a conversation. Have a unique elevator pitch (30 seconds…about the time of a short elevator ride) prepared and ready that will introduce who you are, spark interest, and add value in that person's life. When I was in school, my elevator pitch was "Hi, my name is Marti Reed and I'm a senior student-athlete at UCLA competing in softball with a desire to connect and collaborate with social change-makers and improve my community through real estate development."

2) BUILD RAPPORT

The best way to build rapport is to ask good questions. When you're meeting someone new, they don't want to talk about you. Always remember that it's better to be interested than interesting, so ask them questions and find things you have in common in order to engage in a good conversation. The three magic questions you should know and memorize are: "What made you want to get into…?" "What do you like most about…?" and "If I wanted to get into… which steps would you recommend?"

3) GET THEIR CONTACT INFORMATION

After you've built great rapport by asking good questions and engaging in good conversation, it is perfectly okay to request their contact information in order to continue the relationship. It can sound something like this, "Mr./Ms._____, I really enjoyed speaking with you, and it seems we have some things in common, and I would love to continue this conversation in the future, why don't we exchange information and stay in touch!"

4) STAY IN TOUCH, FOLLOW UP AND FOLLOW THROUGH

This is the most important step in the 4 simple steps to networking. Within 24 hours, immediately send out an email, handwritten letter or thank-you note to your new connection. Do not wait until you see that person again to reconnect. In order to get and maintain relationships with others, you have to continue to follow through with email updates, handwritten letters, holiday/birthday cards, calls, Facebook, LinkedIn, etc. Most people lose out on great connections because they do not follow up and follow through. When networking with people in professional settings, it is your responsibility to keep the relationship going, or they will forget about you (don't take that personal, business professionals are busy and forget).

CHAPTER 15

The Informational Interview

Growing up I always knew I wanted to be an architect. I was passionate about buildings, drawing, and designing. I fell in love with architecture when I was in middle school and it has always been my dream to sell houses and design my own beautiful home. Fast forward some years and here I am today, not an architect, and happy that I'm not. I have absolutely nothing against architecture or architects. I still think architecture is wonderful and I appreciate and love looking at fine buildings, but I know architecture as a profession, is not for me. My skills, values, interests, abilities, and pretty much overall lifestyle are not a true match for that field. I could have dedicated years of school, time, effort and money into mastering the skill of architecture and became an architect, only to find architecture wasn't my thing down the road. Thankfully, informational interviews rescued me from that misuse of time and money, and ultimately changed the course of my life.

Do you know exactly what you want to do with your life professionally? If you're not too sure about your career goals or feel like you lack the relevant knowledge and experience to get the career position you want, I'd highly recommend informational interviews. It's a great way to find out what an industry, company or position is really like (not what you think it's like) by talking to the people that are currently in the careers that you are interested in or considering. Think of it this way, when you go to buy a pair of jeans, you don't just pull the first pair you see off of the rack, you try them on first. When we're choosing a long-term mate, you don't just grab the first person you see walking down the street (at least I hope you don't), and you don't drive away with the first car you see on the lot. We test drive it first. Informational interviews are like trying on careers to see if they fit you.

THE INFORMATIONAL INTERVIEW PROCESS

RESEARCH

Prepare yourself before the interview by doing your homework in advance. Use the internet, LinkedIn, referrals, news articles, secretaries, receptionist, etc. so you don't waste the interviewee's time. Find out everything you can about them before the interview because you shouldn't be asking them simple questions that are easily found on the internet. Know who they are (background, interests, likes/dislikes, etc.), what they've done (accomplishments, projects, etc.), and where and when they did it. You are there to discover the why and the how; you should already know the what, the when and the where. The more you know about the other person, the more they'll think you know about what you're doing.

PRE-HEAT

If you know someone that knows the person you wish to interview and they are in their good graces, have that person put in a word for you. People believe more of what they overhear about you than what they hear directly from you. If you don't have anyone that can pre-heat for you before the interview, create your own pre-heat by sending in your resume, or a personal portfolio before-hand.

BUILD RAPPORT

Use your research to connect with them and make them feel accepted, approved, admired, and important. Start talking about some of the things you know they like, or you know they've done. Mirror their tone, gestures, posture, speed of speech, etc.

DISCOVER AND UNCOVER

This is where the why and how come into place. Ask questions! Ask about their likes, dislikes, ideas, advice. Be interested, not interesting. In other words, you ask the questions and let them do all the talking. You control a conversation by asking questions; you'll dominate a conversation if you're talking too much. Don't dominate the conversation. Prepare your sample questions ahead of time and have at least five "go-to" questions in your head that you can rattle off the bat, but try as best as you can to keep the conversation flowing and build on the information that the person you're interviewing is giving you.

SOME SAMPLE QUESTIONS:

1. How did you get started in…?
2. What were some of the main reasons why you chose to enter this field? What do you consider the most important part of your job and why?

3. Describe a typical day for you on the job?

4. What do you like most about it?

5. What do you like the least about it?

6. If you had to start all over again at my age in your field, what would you do and how would you get started?

7. Where do you see yourself in the next five years?

8. What's next for you?

9. Is there anyone else that you would recommend that I speak to?

10. Are there any internship opportunities coming up and if so, how can I best prepare myself to be the best person for that role?

CLOSE

Make sure to ask for a next step after the interview is over. If this is someone you truly would like to have in your life as a mentor, ask! Say, "I really enjoyed our time together today and I appreciate you sitting down with me to answer my questions. Would it be okay if I stayed in touch with you throughout the year as I embark on my journey?" Ask yourself; is there someone else this person could introduce me to? If so, say, "Based on what we've talked about, would you feel comfortable with introducing me to...?"

The informational interview is by far the fastest way to gain knowledge and clarity in your career goals. We learn faster not by our own experiences, but by the experiences of other people. Listen, learn and implement!

CHAPTER 16

Masterminding

The first time I ever even heard of a Mastermind group was in the timeless book Think and Grow Rich by Napoleon Hill, even though Masterminds have been around forever. (Seriously, even Benjamin Franklin was a part of a Mastermind called Junto). Hill defines a Mastermind as: "The coordination of knowledge and effort of two or more people, who work toward a definite purpose, in the spirit of harmony... No two minds ever come together without thereby creating a third, invisible intangible force, which may be likened to a third mind (the Mastermind)." Basically, the idea of a Mastermind is when you put two or more minds together, you create this super-improved, greater boss of a mind that can help you see further than you've ever seen, reach higher than you've ever imagined and go BIGGER than you could have ever gone alone. The purpose of a Mastermind is to gather together with others to toss around ideas, examine and debate, receive both constructive criticism and inspiration, and support each other while holding each other accountable. In this magical environment, we grow and develop in our personal, spiritual, family, and professional lives.

My first Mastermind group was formed in 2013 and it changed the course of my life. We were a group of four girls who each had the desire to have social impact in one way or another. We met monthly through Skype video conferences and phone calls because we were all in different parts of the world, and it was this group that inspired me to start my blog, and start getting paid to speak. This was the group that helped me overcome my fear, and turn my passions into my full-time career. Since then, I've joined an even larger Mastermind of about 12 people and we actually fly to meet each other for Mastermind weekend retreats every year. After every weekend retreat I leave with a better outlook on life, and feel ready to tackle any obstacle to get to where I want to be. I can honestly say that my Mastermind groups have profoundly helped shape my life and my business. I am so grateful to have such an incredible group of individuals to collaborate and cultivate with, and to hold me accountable. We challenge each other not only to set powerful goals, but also to accomplish them. Everyone in the Mastermind is unique in skill, experience and connections, and brings something that others don't to the table.

When forming a Mastermind group, you must understand that it requires commitment, confidentiality, and willingness to give and receive ideas and advice. You must also support each other with total honesty, trust, respect and compassion. Masterminds are not a class (even though you can vote to bring in guest speakers to your meetings). They are collaborative spaces where you brainstorm together. It is not a group coaching session where one person is facilitating and coaching all of the others. Everyone offers feedback, advice and support. By interacting and sharing your challenges, it's almost certain that someone in your Mastermind will have a solution for you and you may also be able to offer a solution, connection or tactic to help another in the group.

When forming your Mastermind group, here are some key things to remember:

BE CLEAR ABOUT YOUR STRENGTHS, GOALS, AND VISION. I've already mentioned this several times, because it's so important. When you are clear about what you have to offer, what you want to do, and where you are going, it'll be much easier to form a group and see how you can help others and how they can help you.

FIND LIKE-MINDED INDIVIDUALS THAT CHALLENGE YOU. When adding new members to your Mastermind, make sure they are in line with your morals and core values. Look for peers that you can trust; ones that are going to motivate you and help you grow. Invite people to your group that you think are way better than you. Trust me. You don't want to be the smartest person in your Mastermind. For example, whenever I think I got it going on, I get around my Mastermind group and I am extremely humbled because they are absolutely killing it with so many cool things they are up to. Unique backgrounds and strengths will make your group stronger. Surrounding yourself with like-minded individuals that are constantly making positive moves in life will help you step your game up, and keep you in check.

CREATE A STRUCTURE/FORMAT AND ASK FOR A COMMITMENT. Make sure everyone knows what's expected of them. Have a structure to your meetings so they don't run out of control, get off topic, or have one person dominating the entire conversation. There are plenty of Mastermind structures and helpful documents you can find online that will help guide you when creating yours.

If you have not yet joined or started a Mastermind group, I hope you are now convinced how completely advantageous a Mastermind is, and how it can take you to the next level. Once you have the support you need, it will save you many hours of headache and help you overcome challenges no matter where you are in life. You can't truly achieve greatness without the help of others.

CLOSING

A utility player is someone who can play multiple positions well. We see it in sports, and in life—utility playing helps you reach your fullest potential while bringing value to others. Strength in character is one of the most important traits of the utility player. It's in moments of adversity, when your back's against the wall, when you're faced with tough decisions or challenges—those are the moments when your true character comes out. If you focus on leading a life based on your core values, your character will grow strong, and your reputation will follow. Flexibility to embrace opportunities is important as we understand not everything is going to go the way we planned. If we continue to prepare and not wait for everything to be perfect before taking a chance at opportunities, we can go beyond the original things we had planned.

A utility player also knows the importance of having stamina in creating habits. The consistent choices you make on a daily basis become habits that shape your life—choose wisely. A life of sportsmanship involves giving back, treating others with respect, and leaving an impact on this world. And lastly, building your roster by surrounding yourself with positive energy and like-minded people will help you reach your fullest potential. Being the ultimate utility player, focusing on each position—teammate (or family member/friend), student, athlete, professional and community member, will help you create opportunities no matter where you are or what life throws at you.

I'd like to leave you with my top 10 rules for ultimate utility playing in life.

10. Never let fear dominate the way you feel. After all, FEAR just stands for False Evidence Appearing Real.

9. Don't criticize others; it's okay to give second chances. Remember, they're just what we could be under similar circumstances.

8. Value your community and give back to your sisters and brothers. Jackie Robinson said it best: "A life is not important except in the impact it has on others."

7. Use your voice and actions to inspire those around you. Be the team captain of your community by setting the example and following through.

6. Be consistent in your play and never give up, no matter how hard it seems. The future belongs to those who believe in their dreams.

5. Exercise your big plan, because what you're seeking in life is also seeking you. You have the power to decide what you want to do.

4. Ignite your passion with love that's unstoppable. Napoleon Hill said, "Desire backed by faith knows no such things as impossible."

3. The positions you play in life are what shape you. Find balance in physical, intellectual, emotional and spiritual value.

2. Do your mental workouts to keep learning; don't be afraid to open a book. Remember, who you are is much more important than how you look.

1. Build your roster by surrounding yourself with positive people that will help you grow. Because birds of a feather flock together, flock with eagles and let the turkeys go!

It has been my pleasure taking this journey with you. Now you are equipped to live the ultimate utility player life! Never forget, you are fearfully and wonderfully made.

APPENDIX

APPENDIX A

FOR FURTHER READING OR EXPLORATION OF THE CEO'S FROM SPORTS CITED IN CHAPTER 2:

Johnson, Holly. "A look at the link between playing sports and success in business." *CEO Magazine,* The CEO Magazine, 7 May 2018, theceomagazine.com/business/management-leadership/look-link-playing-sports-success-business.

Hamilton, Joan O'C. "Green Crocer." *Stanford Magazine,* August 2007, stanfordmag.org/contents/green-grocer.

Elkins, Kathleen. "These 9 successful CEOs all played sports in college." *Business Insider Australia,* Pedestrian, 19 Feb 2015, businessinsider.com.au/successful-ceos-who-played-sports-in-college-2015-2#ge-ceo-jeffrey-immelt-played-football-for-dartmouth-1.

Glass, Alana. "Ernst & Young Studies The Connection Between Female Executives And Sports." *Forbes,* Forbes Media LLC, 24 June 2013, forbes.com/sites/alanaglass/2013/06/24/ernst-young-studies-the-connection-between-female-executives-and-sports/#1cf7cb6a33a2.

FOR FURTHER READING OR EXPLORATION OF UTILITY PLAYERS THROUGHOUT HISTORY CITED IN CHAPTER 3:

Robinson, Rachel, and Daniels, Lee. *Jackie Robinson: An Intimate Portrait.* Harry N. Abrams; Reissue edition, 2014. Print.

White, Ronald C. A. *Lincoln: A Biography.* New York. Random House Publishing Group, 2010. Print.

Johnson, Earvin "Magic." *32 Ways to Be a Champion in Business.* New York. Three Rivers Press, 2009. Print.

Golightly, Justin. "Ronda Rousey Helps Spread Suicide Awareness With Didi Hirsch." *Ronda Rousey,* Browsey Inc., 31 Mar 2019, rondarousey.com/life/video-ronda-rousey-didi-hirsch-mental-health-services-suicide-prevention-center.

Photo of me with Magic Johnson and my mom, Marcia Reed after I presented at Magic's TMSP Conference in 2014.

APPENDIX B
REFERENCES FOR PART 2: COMMON VALUES OF GREAT UTILITY PLAYERS

Carolsfeld, Julius Schnorr von Carolsfeld. *Treasury of Bible Illustrations: Old and New Testaments.* Dover Publications, Inc., 1999. Print.

Bed Making Habits:

Block, Logan. "Happy National Make Your Bed Day! See Our Survey Results." *Sleepopolis,* OnePoll, 12 Sept 2018, sleepopolis.com/news/happy-national-make-your-bed-day-see-our-survey-results.

REFERENCES FOR PART 3: UTILITY TRAINING AND POSITIONING

Chapman, Gary. *The 5 Love Languages: The Secret to Love That Lasts.* Chicago. Northfield Publishing, 2015. Print.

Take the quiz and learn your love language at www.5lovelanguages.com.

APPENDIX C
BUILDING A PERSONAL PORTFOLIO

Building a personal portfolio (or book of achievements) is a great way to pre-heat yourself for job or scholarship opportunities. I am including detailed instructions beyond what I provided in the book. Please take the time to try and build your personal portfolio, and feel free to email me at marti@themartireed.com if you'd like to see a copy of mine, or if you have any questions!

You Will Need:
- 1 and ½ inch 3 ring binder with the pockets on the front and

back to slide papers in
- Plastic Sheet Protectors
- Scanner
- Computer with Microsoft Word, PowerPoint, or Keynote
- Printer
- Blue Ink Pen
- Awards, pictures, certificates, letters of recommendation, newspaper clippings and anything else you want to show off about yourself

STEP 1

Collect the awards, pictures, letters of recommendation, certificates, newspaper clippings, etc. that you want to include in your personal portfolio.

STEP 2

Scan and save them onto your computer. If they are already online or on the computer, then you can skip this step…lucky you!

STEP 3

Layout the items that are now on your computer into a Microsoft Word, PowerPoint presentation, or Keynote. Follow the visual page-by-page instructions for layout ideas.

STEP 4

Print the pages on a color printer.

STEP 5

Place your most important and impressive portfolio pages in clear plastic sheet protectors and place those in your 1 and ½" binder.

STEP 6

Put a copy of your resume in the last pocket at the end of your binder.

Create your own personal portfolio to give potential mentors, employers or people an idea of who you are, your background and credentials, and the value you can bring to any company or organization.

ACKNOWLEDGEMENTS

I have to start by thanking my Lord and Savior, Jesus Christ (for real, for real). None of this would be possible without my faith.

Next up…my family. I know I already dedicated the book to them, but they have been my biggest support system and sounding board throughout this whole process, so they get another shout out. My father—Big Marty. Thank you for instilling a work ethic in me that seems crazy to most, but absolutely necessary to reach my big, hairy audacious goals and dreams. My sister and bestie, Rae. You have been willing to listen and share all of my work. You're my number one "hype-woman" and if this thing bombs or takes-off… I know you'll have my back either way. My brother, Kez Reed. You have been willing and able to pick up the phone whenever I call to offer me advice and tough love—from book editing to marketing. Thanks for caring and helping me succeed, always. And last but certainly not least, my role model, my hero, my mother, Marcia Reed. From reading early drafts, to correcting my grammar (although I'm sure I didn't get it up to your level of perfection), and giving me feedback every step of the way. Thank you so much. I appreciate you for always being there no matter what. I am eternally grateful to each of you!

To everyone at Positive Coaching Alliance (too many names to list)—thank you! It's not easy to manage a full-time job and write a book on the side, but you have supported me, encouraged me and taught me so much. Thanks for continuing to fill my "emotional-tank," enabling me to serve such an important and impactful mission!

My teammates and coaches at UCLA. Thank you for providing me with an amazing college experience. Truly some of the best years of my life. Thanks for shaping me into the person I am today and giving me so many stories and life lessons that I've included in this book.

A very special thanks to Charlie Gallagher, Dr. Bill and the rest of my LEAP family! The LEAP program has had such a tremendous impact on my life and the biggest concepts in this book.

To the Office of Awesome—my brand architects! Rebecca and Leah, you both worked with me to recreate and launch The Marti Reed brand. You helped foster the idea of the Utility Player. You saw things in me that I wasn't able to see and I am forever grateful for your support, guidance and expertise!

Writing a book is MUCH harder than I thought, and re-writing the book was even harder. To my substantial editor, Delina Pryce McPhaull who was referred to me by my mentor, Jonathan Sprinkles, THANK YOU! You challenged me (literally deleted entire chapters), you elevated me, and you worked very well with me throughout the process. I so appreciate you! Jerome Vincent Carter with Inspiration52. Thank you so much!

To my Pastor Erwin and first lady Joanne Guevara, and the rest of my New Dawn Christian Village family…thank you for being my caring congregation of spirit led believers always drawing me closer to Christ.

Last but not least…my roster! The mentors, family and friends by my side. I see you. I thank you. I love you.

ABOUT THE AUTHOR

Marti Reed grew up in Long Beach, California and played softball at UCLA from 2008-2012, where she graduated with a degree in Sociology and a minor in Global Studies. During her time at UCLA, she won a National Championship with the softball team in 2010 after scoring the tying run in the championship game to eventually beat the Arizona Wild Cats in extra innings.

Marti was able to leave her mark as a highly decorated student athlete — including leader of the Bruin Athletic Council, Athletes in Action Christian club, Afrikan Student Union, Alumni Scholarship Committee, Student Athlete Mentors, a 2011 Bruin Leadership Award, UCLA Ralph Bunche scholarship, Lew and Edi Wasserman Alumni Scholarship, Chancellor's Service Award, and a spot on the Director's Honor Roll every quarter of her academic career which all led her to eventually achieve 2012 UCLA Senior of the Year.

Marti now serves as the Development Manager for a non-profit called Positive Coaching Alliance (PCA) promoting "better athletes, better people" by teaching life lessons through sports. Since joining PCA, Marti has helped launch their Los Angeles Chapter, partnering with the major sports franchises in Los Angeles including the LA Lakers, LA Dodgers, LA Clippers, LA Sparks, LA Galaxy, and FOX Sports. Marti is also the fit model for Easton Fastpitch to help softball gear be the most efficient and attractive for young females. Marti continues to coach softball clinics and camps across the nation. She spends time volunteering and speaking for organizations such as the Magic Johnson Foundation, the LEAP foundation and the YBA (Youth Business Alliance). As a coach, national speaker and mentor, she specializes in working with athletes prepare for life outside their game with the same commitment they brought to their sport. Marti's mission is to help students reach their fullest potential and make positive contributions throughout their lives.